# BOBBITT

## 5'2 GIANT
## HANDLING THE ODDS

**SHANNON BOBBITT**

# DEDICATION

I would like to dedicate this book to everyone who believed in me when I didn't believe in myself. I want to also dedicate this book to all of the youth who are in doubt and facing seemingly insurmountable odds in life. If I can make it, you can make it.

Dreams are worth chasing.

Thank you.

# ACKNOWLEDGMENTS

I would like to thank God for all of the blessings I have, including being able to make a difference in others' lives. I would like to thank everyone who helped me birth my first book. I would like to thank all of my family, friends, and fans for their love and support. Special thanks to Coach Summitt for giving me an opportunity—that scholarship changed my life. And last but certainly not least, I would like to thank my parents. I love you both with all of my heart. The times I wanted to give up, you never let me. I will never be the woman you are, Mommy, and I may never find a man like you, Daddy, but I can promise that I will come as close as possible. You both are my rocks. If it weren't for your tough love, guidance, and wisdom, I would not be the woman I am today.

# CONTENTS

# FOREWORD

This upcoming season in 2016 will mark my sixteenth and final season playing in the WNBA for the Indiana Fever. It will actually stand to be the end of my basketball career, and I will be venturing on to whatever God has for me next. Through my years of playing for the Indiana Fever, there have been some great players who have impacted my life in some way or another, one of those being—yes, you guessed it—Shannon Bobbitt.

I remember the first time I saw and heard about Shannon, she was on her way from Trinity Valley Community College to head to my alma mater, the University of Tennessee in Knoxville. Everyone raved about how big she played on the court while standing at five feet two inches tall. But what she didn't have in height, she made up for in game. She was an exciting player to watch and definitely one that would have your adrenaline sky high from the moves that she made for herself and/or her teammates who were on the court with her. With all of her talent, and by leading the charge from the point guard position, she helped the University of Tennessee win two National Championships her last two years of college.

I had an opportunity to get to know Shannon a little bit during college, but our friendship really got stronger after her stint in Los Angeles with the Sparks was over and she was signed to play for the Indiana Fever. When I think about Shannon and her time with the Fever, I think about our late night McDonald's runs because, win or lose, I wanted to get French fries and talk about whatever game we just played. I think about my buddy who I could just walk around with talking basketball or life. I think about this young lady who was trying to find herself, and while she wore this hard shell on the outside, she may have been one of the softest, sweetest people on the inside.

I admire the commitment and dedication that Shannon has had in getting her story out. She has been working on telling the world her story and inspiring so many young men and women to follow their dreams "against the odds." This book offers insight into her life both on and off the court and how she has been able to succeed with a strong supporting cast in her family, fueled by a determination to be the best along the way. I am so honored to be a part of her journey, and I know that you will enjoy reading about a true champion.

Enjoy!

Best wishes and God bless,

*Tamika Catchings*
*WNBA, Indiana Fever*
*Founder, Catch the Stars Foundation*

# PROLOGUE

My heart pounded. Panic overcame me. I couldn't breathe; I gasped desperately for air. The fears crept up on me like a thief in the night. I felt helpless. My mind raced a million miles a minute, going in every direction. What happens if I fall right here? What if no one rescues me?

That was my first anxiety attack. I didn't let it hold me back, though. I couldn't. I kept thinking, "This is all in my mind. I have to make it—I can't stop now."

Not all dreams are fiction. They hold some truth, a message to reality. Dreams start with a thought. Then, you make that dream a promise to yourself. I wanted to make it to the WNBA. Basketball was my passion, but I faced difficulties along the way that threatened my dream, even when I took the road less traveled.

Everyone starts out with a dream. I had my own.

# 1. PLANT YOUR FEET

I was born Shannon Denise Bobbitt on a cold December day in 1985, before the first snowfall of the season, in the Bronx, New York. I enjoyed growing up with my siblings; we had so much fun. When I was four years old, there were seven of us: four boys and three girls. My brothers—Anthony Jr., Tyrone, Stevie, and Eugene—were older than me. My sisters were Shareese and Jennifer; Shareese was the oldest, Jennifer the youngest. We all got along well and had a tight bond. Growing up with four older brothers made me a tomboy, but Shareese and my mother, Linda, provided some balance. My brothers toughened me up and taught me how to hold my ground. I was somewhat aggressive and competitive by nature, which helped build the foundation for the determination that drove me to succeed.

We lived in a three-bedroom apartment for a time, and with such a large family, we began to feel crowded. We needed a bigger place, and there was an apartment available one street down from where we lived, so we moved to Cypress Avenue. My family and I adjusted to our new home right away. It wasn't the best area, but we handled it well because we had the right intentions.

My father, Anthony Sr., and my mother worked extremely hard to support and protect us. There were times we would hear gunshots; people were getting shot in front of our apartment building. It was frightening. Sometimes I'd awaken in the middle of the night from the exploding sounds of a gun and go to my parents' bedroom for safety. We couldn't play in front of our building, because drug dealers ruled the area.

Anthony Jr. had a friend whose brother was known for shooting people in the neighborhood. He once put a gun to my brother's chest and threatened him. Anthony Jr. was only twelve at the time—that's when he decided to stay away from those guys. Shareese, Jennifer, and I always found some way to have fun inside, because it was simply too dangerous to go outside. We couldn't go out without our parents because we were still so young and weren't able look out for ourselves. Although we didn't make many friends in the neighborhood, we had each other.

I was extremely close with my sisters. Shareese was very kind and funny. Being older, she'd watch over Jennifer and me. Jennifer was still a baby when we moved—only twenty-three months old—but she was a smart and happy child.

On July 17, 1989, a terrible tragedy befell our family. It was a hot summer day; the neighborhood was filled with people, loud and cheerful voices fading in and out, the atmosphere filled with music and warmth. I remember a blue sky, bright sun, laughter, and heat. In a split second, all of that changed.

We were cooped up at home. Mom was at work, and Dad was due at work by two in the afternoon. He was waiting for the babysitter to arrive before he left. He didn't want to be late, as his boss was strict about absentees and late arrivals.

As the clock neared two, Dad became edgy and impatient. The babysitter was running behind schedule, and he had to leave or he'd be late as well. He told one of my brothers to watch us until the babysitter arrived, and then he went off to work.

During the time we were at home alone, Jennifer saw my brothers approach the fire escape to talk to some girls who lived one floor above us. No one was paying attention to Jennifer; unseen, she climbed on the radiator cover and began to walk out onto the fire escape.

Jennifer stood up and held onto one of the metal bars, and before anyone noticed, she slipped and fell to the concrete, some thirty to forty feet below. She had fallen out of the window from the fourth floor.

Paramedics arrived immediately and worked to save my sister. She was moved to the front of the building, where the ambulance was located. My mother was coming down the street and had no idea what was happening. A neighbor informed her: "Linda, I think your daughter just fell out of the window," she said, her face creased from worry.

My mom was dumbfounded. "No, not my daughter," she replied. "It can't be my daughter. Are you sure?" She started walking faster, heart racing as the panic took over. Her hands trembled in fear as she caught sight of the large group of people gathered around an ambulance right in front of our building. When she saw that it was true, my mom was frozen in disbelief.

Police detectives got involved. My dad didn't know what had happened until he returned home from work, and the detectives were waiting to question him about the incident. Dad rushed to the hospital, and the doctors told him Jennifer was stable for now. Nevertheless, Mom and Dad stayed with Jennifer at the hospital for three days straight while our babysitter cared for the rest of us.

It was absolute agony—waking up every morning, hoping my sister would get better. It was the most stressful situation my family and I had ever handled. My parents neither ate, nor slept, nor worked. All we could do was pray and stay calm and wish for the best. I thought about how Jennifer looked after she had fallen, sobbing and bleeding on the ground, the crowd gaping at her. I couldn't imagine what she would have been feeling. Mom stayed at Jennifer's bedside day and night, talking to her, whispering, "It's mommy and daddy, Jenny. Fight, baby, fight. Fight."

But three days of fighting were enough. The doctors told my mom and dad they could go home to rest since Jennifer seemed to be okay. As soon as they got home, however, they received a phone call from the hospital saying they should come back right away. Jennifer couldn't fight any longer. She was too small to survive such a hard hit to the ground. She was bleeding internally, and her heartbeat was abnormally fast. The medicine the doctors had administered to slow her heart rate hadn't worked. Jennifer didn't have much longer to live.

My mom panicked and started blaming herself. She just wanted my little sister to fight as long and hard as she could. She was broken. In a way, we all were.

Jennifer was pronounced dead on July 19, 1989. She died two days before my dad's birthday and exactly one month before her own. My little sister, my friend, was gone. The laughter that had brightened our house was gone.

Being one of the biggest ordeals we'd ever gone through, it tore our family apart. There was heartbreaking commotion that day. My family was so distraught, I didn't know if we'd be able to survive it. It felt like life was over—like the pain would never end. We tried to move on, though things weren't the same, and never would be. We were in shock, and the family collectively descended into a deep depression. I was only four years old, but I felt Jennifer's absence like the emptiness of a ghost. Though it was summer, it felt cold in the house—dull and dark. I saw the tears in my parents' eyes and felt sad, even defeated. No one smiled or laughed.

Jennifer's death inevitably changed our lives. We questioned God and asked why this had happened— why she had been taken from us. It felt like my parents were in grief and anguish forever, though they tried their best to hold their composure in front of us and managed to keep the family tight and together.

I think of my sister every day, talking to her through prayer and asking her to watch over the family. I just wish we were all together again. One day we will be. Losing a family member, especially one so young and innocent, is an indescribable feeling. We never thought something like that would happen. We never did understand why Jennifer was taken from us. If I could, I would give up my biggest passion in life—basketball—just to have my sister back.

The good things about my time in New York City were the opportunities I felt I would have growing up there. There were always places to go and things to do. I loved the bright lights and big buildings.

The parks were very entertaining for my siblings and me; we would play tag every time we had the opportunity. The variety of food available in New York was amazing. I was used to eating home-cooked meals, which I loved, but I also had the opportunity to eat authentic Spanish, Italian, and Chinese foods. Personally, I love New York, even now. There is no better city to me. It's one of the most diverse cities in the world, rich in culture, and there's always something new to see. New York has a great variety of food, any kind of cuisine you could possibly want. The city is known for its great sport teams—the Jets, Giants, Knicks, Brooklyn Nets, Rangers, Islanders, Mets, Liberty, and, of course, the Yankees. For me, basketball is the true sport of the city. It rules, especially in the summer. But it was in Forest, Mississippi, where I first picked up a basketball.

In 1990, my parents decided it would be good to get away from New York City and travel to Mississippi to help free our minds and heal ourselves from heartbreak. My father's parents lived there, so we prepared to visit.

Within the first week of staying with my grandparents, my mom and dad unexpectedly decided that we should move to the south. My Aunt Shirley kept us for a week while my parents returned to New York to get our furniture and belongings. It was a rough beginning, but we eventually found a home to rent, and Dad started at a new job.

Wages earned in Mississippi were different than in New York, and money didn't go very far. My dad worked at the local hospital, and Mom worked at a Kentucky Fried Chicken. We enrolled in school, and it was an entirely different experience. At first, it was even a little funny, hearing everyone's southern accents, but I then realized my own accent was funny to them. Luckily, I made friends quickly. We lived in a complex that was peaceful. There were no shootings or violence, so we had much more playtime outside. I felt truly free.

On a summer day in 1992, Dad and my brothers headed to the park to play basketball. This was a regular occurrence, since we didn't have a backyard. I'd been looking for a sport to play, so I asked my dad if I could tag along, and he agreed. I stayed on the sidelines for the first few minutes, watching the game and cheering everyone on. But the basketball bounced my way, and my first instinct was to take it and start dribbling.

I handled the ball as if I'd been playing for a long time. I felt the ease of it instantly. It was enough to get Dad's attention, and from that moment my father knew I was going to be something special.

Soon, I began carrying a ball everywhere I went, just to practice. Eventually, I came to love and enjoy the sport. Basketball started to mean everything to me. I couldn't go a day without playing or watching basketball. It became a part of my daily routine and a part of my life. I wanted to return to the park again and again to play.

My parents had worked long and hard, saved enough money, and finally decided it was time to buy a home. In late 1993, they found a fairly nice brick house. We finally had our own yard, and I had a place to practice basketball. Dad would barbecue often and invite family and friends, and our cousins would often come over to play. We were content, though it was a struggle to put food on the table and try to pay the mortgage and utility bills. We had moved to escape the pain of losing my sister, but we didn't know that we'd be in for more pain and hardship here.

On New Year's Day, my dad was putting a transmission in his van with help from his brother, Calvin. After completing the job, Dad took Uncle Calvin back to my grandparents' house and drove around to make sure the transmission was working properly. Afterwards, he decided to go to the grocery store to get a beer and call it a day.

Once Dad entered the store, he heard the radio scanner mention a fire at 820 Southwest Street. He knew that was right across the street from my grandparents' house.

He drove to their neighborhood and ran down the street to the house, where he saw Uncle Calvin lying down with smoke coming from his body. His hands were smoldering, his ears melted from the top. Dad asked him about grandma and granddad, but Calvin said they didn't make it. His throat was closing, cutting off his oxygen supply. Paramedics had to force an oxygen tube down his throat before rushing him to a burn unit in Texas. Uncle Calvin was saved after long-term treatment and surgery. This was yet another painful experience and loss for the family. My grandparents were wonderful people. We also lost a niece in the fire, who was just over a year old.

My parents tried to make life as happy as possible for us, but times were hard. My father lost his job at the hospital, where he worked as a housekeeper, security guard, janitor, and a runner to get supplies from the emergency room for doctors. At one point, as he was juggling his many different roles for work, he was busy with a housekeeping assignment, so he couldn't get the supplies to the doctors right away, and they fired him. Afterwards, he worked as an auto mechanic for two years. He then began working for Hughes Aircraft, which was a job he enjoyed. My mom worked for a chicken-processing plant while continuing part-time at KFC.

We were doing well until my mom got sick and was told she needed surgery right away. We went to the hospital in Jackson, Mississippi, where they said Mom must have surgery the next morning or she would not live. The doctor said she might not even live through the surgery. My dad decided it would be best to fly Mom back to New York to be seen by a specialist and get a second opinion. My mom's family in New York helped fly her back. I was worried about my mom; she was away from us, and I didn't know what to expect.

When the doctors in New York saw my mother, they decided on the proper procedure to follow. She

still needed surgery, but it didn't need to take place
the next day as the other doctors had recommended;
it would take place a month later. There was no rush
for the surgery. The doctors in New York gave us
some peace of mind.

After the surgery, Mom let us know she was fine,
much to our relief. But she decided she wanted to
move back to the Big Apple. Meanwhile, my father
was finished at Hughes Aircraft. The contract
deadline was close, and the project was a success.
Hughes Aircraft began layoffs, and Dad was on the
list. It was a setback for our family, but he had a
second job as a maintenance worker for an
apartment complex as a backup. When Mom
decided it was time to move back to New York,
Dad thought it was the right decision, even though it
wasn't planned.

The maintenance job my dad had on the side for
extra income usually sent a check in the mail, which
arrived on Tuesdays. The weekend Dad decided to
leave, the check unexpectedly arrived—right on

time to help with the move. Dad drove us back to New York. At the time, the newest addition to my family, my little brother Chris, was only about two years old, and I had just turned six.

Once we arrived in New York, we went to stay with my mom's mother at the Public Housing Developments, better known as "the projects." My father got back his former job working in the warehouse and driving trucks. I often went to the courts behind the buildings and played sports. Things finally appeared to be falling into place. We were welcomed at first, but not for long.

I made a name for myself right away. I played touch football and began playing basketball. I must admit, I was outstanding to not have had any practice or training. Although I always had fun outside, returning to my grandmother's house wasn't something I looked forward to; I felt unwelcome there.

Dad was at work early one morning making a delivery. On his way downstairs with a hand truck, he slipped and felt something pop in his back. He couldn't move and had to be rushed to the hospital. An MRI showed damage to his spine, with a bulging disc, an annular tear in his disc and several herniated discs, which kept him out of work. He eventually lost his job and couldn't work any place else with his condition.

While staying with my grandmother, I attended P.S. 43. I was so excited but nervous at the same time. I didn't know what to expect from the teachers or even from my classmates. I just wanted to make friends and adjust quickly so the school year would be easier for me.

The first day of classes was actually interesting, because I realized a lot of the people who stayed in the same projects as I did went to my school. My sister was in the school as well, so I was somewhat comforted when I would see her at lunch or in the hallways. I was a very shy girl and had self-esteem issues growing up. I always doubted myself because I was never confident in things I said or did. I was afraid of being laughed at or being told I was wrong. Rejection and failure were constant points of fear for me. I didn't have reasons to be doubtful; I just wanted to make sure I was right in everything I did or said. On the other hand, I had many leadership qualities and was very self-disciplined growing up. But confidence is the key to having high self-esteem, and not caring what people thought or said about me was hard. I did care. I never wanted people to look down on me. I never enjoyed speaking, because I didn't think I would sound right or make any sense to the people listening. I was tired of transferring from school to school. I was friendly, easy to approach and talk to, but really shy, too. On that first day, we had to introduce ourselves in class and share so everyone could get to know each other. I shared that I played basketball.

I immediately got attention from the guys, because they couldn't believe a girl would say she played basketball. One guy made a smart comment and said that girls couldn't play ball and that I couldn't beat him. I smiled and said, "OK, where is the court and when is recess?" My classmates and the teacher started laughing, and everyone started to talk with me.

I gained friends just from my short introduction and retaliatory comment to the boy. I sat down and felt a little more comfortable because I had made my classmates laugh, and all I could hear was the girls and boys whispering, saying they had money on the girl—me. I was smiling so widely inside. I couldn't wait until recess. Unfortunately, since it was the beginning of the school year, the class times were short. There was no recess time, so we couldn't play that day. When the school year started with the full day schedule, we played, and I won the game. After that day, I was the talk of my school.

While staying with my grandmother, we had many unpleasant incidents with her. She drank and would become disrespectful and insolent, but if my parents said anything, we would be told to move out. My brother Tyrone went back to Mississippi to get away from the difficulty of living with her. Once, she even turned on me.

Every morning I woke up early and went to the store to buy little snacks for my cousin and me. One morning my grandmother asked me where I was going so early.

"To the store," I replied.

"How'd you get the money?" she asked.

"My daddy's pants pocket," I said.

"Did you ask him?" she scolded.

"No, because he sleeps," I responded. "Besides, I always take money out like that, so he won't mind."

I'd take no more than a dollar, but I guess back in those days a dollar was a lot, because my grandmother started screaming at me. She grabbed me with such force that I instantly became afraid I'd be hurt. I started crying and immediately went to tell my parents what had happened.

My parents confronted her, reminding her that I was not her child and forbidding her from ever putting her hands on me again. That was when we realized it really was time to move out.

Later that day, I went outside to play ball and free my mind when a young man came to me and said I had a really good handle and that I should get into a basketball tournament. He gave me a number for a person named Pee Wee, who was known for holding basketball tournaments for girls.

I spoke to my dad and gave him the number, and he promptly called and got me registered. We got the address and took the train to East 96th Street, but we then learned that the place was actually on the west end, so we walked through Central Park to get there.

Dad knocked on the door of a big Catholic church. A nun came to the door and informed us that Pee

Wee was on 115th Street between Fifth and Lenox avenues. We traveled there and saw Pee Wee sitting at a table, signing up players for the tournament. My dad walked up to the table.

The first thing Pee Wee asked was, "Does she have handle?"

"Yeah," Dad replied.

"Take her over to that group," Pee Wee said.

I went to the group where the short players were – the point guards. I played well: it was all natural skill and talent and just happened. A man named Coach Mark noticed me and asked my dad if I could play with his team. Dad agreed, and the games began.

I started enjoying the sport when I was seven years old, but I fell in love with the game and started taking it seriously at the age of twelve. I began to practice every day. Basketball was my priority growing up, along with doing well in school, and I never let family, friends, or boys distract me from my goals or keep me from reaching success. Even though I made a few wrong decisions along the way, I knew they would not mess up my goals for basketball or school. If I liked a guy and he wanted to spend time with me, I made him come pass me the ball to ensure I handled priorities before spending time with him. I made sure my homework was done before going to a friend's home or even outside to hang out and chill. I had my mind made up at an early age that I wanted to be successful and make a better life for my parents and myself. When I was thirteen years old I was doing things and saying things adults would. I didn't have my parents waking me up in morning or telling me to go to sleep. I knew that was mandatory and it was a priority to go to school to learn and graduate. I never was a normal kid; I was old at a young age. I always felt the need to keep my guard up and stay disciplined, because I knew that if I slacked, I might not be able to bounce back. I made good decisions in my life overall, and looking back on it all I wouldn't change a thing. I wouldn't want to see what things would be like if I hadn't gone to school, or if I had stayed with the street boyfriends or hung with friends late into the nights. Whatever would make me happy in the long run or make my future brighter—that's what I did first, before anything else. With basketball, I did several different layup drills with my right and left hands on the court. I worked on my ball-handling skills, dribbling around cones up and down the court, and practiced shooting the ball from all different angles. I practiced multiple times a day, and my workouts lasted about two to three hours each. I was young and had the energy to play basketball all the time.

Things developed quickly. I played against guys and was truly competitive. Spectators were shocked to see a small girl playing against boys, but I feared no one. I crossed them over and took the ball away from them. Some were sweating hard as I played defense. The boys would actually get mad because they felt embarrassed to see a young female outplaying them—especially someone who had just started.

I never played a full game of basketball, though. I was always on the sideline, wishing for my chance to play. Soon, I became known as the best female ballplayer around. There were rumors of other girls saying they could beat me, but I just continued having fun and getting better, knowing the summer was drawing to a close. Playing ball helped me deal with problems at home.

But the summer slipped past, and eventually the summer tournaments ended. I no longer had basketball to occupy my mind. I wanted a place of our own to live, because we had to take a lot of mistreatment from my grandmother while living with her. Her reasoning was that there were too many kids in the house.

The event that eventually changed things was when my grandmother called the police on my parents. She told them she wanted us out, but the police said they couldn't do anything to make us leave because we had done nothing wrong. I was very sad and disappointed that my own grandmother would treat us so badly every time she had a few too many drinks. I saw my mom crying and my dad angry, and I immediately thought things were going bad. I was a sensitive kid.

My grandmother would start arguments with my parents just because that was her personality when she drank. All I would hear was screaming and doors being slammed. This even happened on school and work days, and I would immediately jump out of bed to see what was going on. I'd be crying and telling my parents I couldn't sleep, suggesting that we leave and telling them that I was scared. They would assure me that things were okay and tell me to get some rest and that nothing would happen to them or me.

My grandmother would wake us up yelling and telling us to get out of the house at two or three in the morning sometimes. It was very uncomfortable, because we never knew what kind of day or night to expect when my grandmother drank. Sometimes things would even get violent. But my dad always made sure we were all safe. When it came to his family, he was a protective man. The outbursts by my grandmother became so frequent that my parents thought it would be best to go elsewhere, because otherwise someone might get hurt. My great-grandmother, who was close to my mother, also thought it would be best if we moved out.

In 1996, after putting up with her mother's abuse for a year, my mother went to a shelter because we couldn't find an apartment. This was our first out-of-the-ordinary experience. It was just my mom and the kids. Dad couldn't stay with us because he and Mom weren't actually married at the time. A couple had to be legally married to stay in the shelter, so Dad had to go stay with family members.

Living conditions at the shelter were horrendous. We were checked every time we left or entered the building, and no cameras were allowed. We even had curfews. When we were given a room to sleep in, the door hung by one hinge and roaches crawled all around. The room had mold and a stench to it. The whole place was filthy. I didn't understand why they let people sleep in these places.

Mom went out and bought bleach to sanitize our area. We were catching stomach viruses and dealing with rude attitudes from the staff, who had no concerns about the conditions of our room. During my weeks in the shelter, I didn't have the opportunity to play much basketball, because there weren't any courts nearby. We often visited the homes of our relatives for several hours, so I played basketball during that time until we had to be back at the shelter.

My parents both agreed that my siblings and I did not have to attend school for a few days because of our situation, suggesting that we refrain from going until things got better. I was relieved; I would've been embarrassed if my schoolmates knew I was living in a shelter. Eventually, though, we had to return to school because it was taking a long time to find our own apartment, and we were missing too many days.

Eventually it was just my sister, my younger brother Chris, my mom, and I living together in the shelter. Since my sister and I were the youngest, and girls, and Chris was too young to be separated from my mom, she didn't trust anyone with us. Like Dad, my older brothers went to stay with other relatives. Since they were older, Mom knew they'd be safe. There were nights I couldn't sleep at all. With my brothers and father not with us, I felt no security. We never thought we'd be homeless, especially not for weeks. It was one of the worst struggles of my life, but I knew we would find a way through it. It was rough, but we had no choice other than to stay positive.

When Mom told Dad she couldn't take it anymore, Dad spoke to his sister, Aunt Mary, and asked if we could stay with her. He told her he didn't mind if he and Mom slept on the floor. Aunt Mary agreed.

Getting to my aunt's apartment was a journey. Dad had to take the train to Brooklyn to pick us up. It was a stormy night with harsh winds and blinding rain, but we were anxious to get out of that filthy place. We had several large plastic bags holding our belongings.

As we walked, the wind blew so hard that I felt as if I were about to be swept off my feet. Dad carried my little brother as we fought the wind and rain to get to the train station.

Once we made it, we sat in the deserted station waiting for the train. Feeling cold and wet, we were quiet, just waiting for a warm place to rest our minds and bodies. Chris handled it well. He didn't cry; he simply wanted the same thing everyone else wanted. We were cold, but we were on our way to a home—that's what mattered at the time.

On our way uptown to the Bronx, people on the train looked at us with pity. My parents felt embarrassed to be homeless. It was strange to have people staring as if they couldn't believe the sight of us.

Aunt Mary didn't have much room in her apartment, but she did the best she could to make us comfortable. Mom and Dad slept on the floor, while Shareese, Chris, and I slept in the bed. As a result of moving in with Aunt Mary, I had to switch schools and began attending school in the Bronx on Nelson Avenue. I was sad about having to change schools because things didn't work out at my grandmother's home. I didn't even get to finish the school year at P.S. 43, but luckily I was only in the fourth grade.

My mom took me to register for the school, which was about a ten-minute walk from where we lived. Once again, I had to meet and greet a new teacher and classmates. I didn't know anyone in the school. I was the new kid on the block. I had to introduce myself to the class, and this time I didn't mention I played ball. I was so shy and sad that I had to change schools that I just wanted to say my name and sit down.

Thankfully, my classmates were really friendly. I didn't have a hard time adjusting to my new school. The first few days were rough because I had nobody to talk to or walk to school with since my sister attended another school with my cousin. I was so sad that I had to be alone, but I couldn't do anything about it, so I did what I had to do. After awhile things got better, and I made friends and did well in my classes. That was the big picture, and the only thing that mattered.

## 2. LONG STORY SHORT

I was now eleven years old, and we still didn't have our own home. I still loved playing basketball, especially since I knew I had a gift from God that could change my life forever. I knew I could be really good if I worked hard and had passion for the sport. I commanded a lot of attention and respect; I could impact a game, even being so small. Basketball would also allow me to have an impact on others' lives and motivate them to do well and be successful. With all the disruptions, I had to learn and adapt by observing my family's struggles and the pain we endured. I knew I wanted to make things better, and I didn't want to live a hard life all the time.

We started moving often. Every time we moved, I switched to a new school. That was one of the hardest things for me as a child. After bouncing around from home to home, we finally paid our dues to get our own place.

A family friend had a vacant apartment that she wanted to sublease to my mother and father. They jumped on the offer, and after Dad paid the first month's rent, we picked up our furniture from Mississippi and moved into the apartment.

Dad was worried about my brother, Tyrone, who was still in Mississippi. He moved back there while we were still staying with my grandmother and my mother was getting treatment for her ongoing condition. Tyrone wanted to stay in the south because he enjoyed living there. He had a girlfriend that lived in Mississippi, whom he didn't want to leave.

When Dad went to Mississippi to get the furniture, he got in touch with Tyrone. My brother had lost weight to the point where his jaws were sunken in. Dad was upset that his relatives apparently hadn't been properly taking care of his son and had left him practically homeless and starving. He picked up Tyrone, retrieved the furniture, and left town. They had a long trip back home, but made it safely. Everything my parents had gone through in New York with family members on my mother's side, being treated badly and abused verbally, my brother had also gone through with my father's side of the family. My dad was a man who always wanted everyone to be happy and to get along. He wanted to make sure everyone was safe. He was always thinking about how my brother was doing alone in Mississippi. Everything happens for a reason, though. We got a break on finding an apartment, and my dad had a reason to go south, and the family was finally all together again.

After the furniture arrived, my Aunt Robin contacted my mother. She told Mom that a manager from a housing project had a vacant apartment available for us to see. We were ready to move into the current apartment, but some of the furniture was too wide to go through the doorway. It was frustrating, and not being able to fit all of our furniture into the apartment we'd already paid for felt like a waste of money and effort. So Mom set up an appointment with the housing manager to see the other apartment.

We decided to take the other apartment right away. It had four bedrooms, which gave us enough room to spread out and relax. I was excited about finally having our own place. Constantly moving from school to school every few months had been difficult for me. In the course of one year, I had transferred schools three times because we didn't have a stable residence. I never had enough time to settle in or get comfortable enough to make friends. With our own place, I felt as if we were finally somewhere I could permanently call home.

We moved in on Thanksgiving Day. Soon after, I began attending P.S. 207 on Lenox Avenue. I made new friends, played basketball during lunch breaks, and best of all, I had a good home to return to after school.

The following year, I started the fifth grade. It was around September 1996, so it was still warm enough to go outside for recess. I was nervous about my first day and again had to introduce myself to the other students. I waited for recess all through class, and we finally went outside at about 12:30 p.m. I watched first, studying my opponents. They were playing two-on-two, three-on-three. Then, I yelled from the sideline that I'd be next. The guys just looked at me and started laughing, but said I could play.

When the game finally ended, recess was almost over. Our opponents scored the first three points. I was forced to play defense for three straight possessions. This was upsetting, because I wanted to prove to the boys that girls could play on both ends, too. Finally, they missed the shot that would have given them four points. Now, it was my turn.

I put on a show. I did moves you would have to see to believe. I was crossing over between my legs, bouncing the ball behind my back. My team quickly went up by five points. Other girls stopped what they were doing to come watch me play. They looked amazed because I was aggressive and quick. I had the guys arguing with each other about who was going to stop me. Recess time was up, but the game wasn't settled. After the game ended, it was all the entire school could talk about—the girl from the basketball game at recess, the new girl, Shannon Bobbitt.

I was pleased that I'd played well and earned respect from my classmates. Now, the guys looked forward to putting me on their team. The next day, I went outside on lunch break to play basketball, and my teacher noticed me. She approached me and said I had a special gift. When my parents came to pick me up after school, my teacher told them I should be in a private school because of my talent.

P.S. 207 didn't have a girls' team, and my teacher explained that Mt. Carmel had a nice basketball program for both boys and girls. This would help me be part of an organized team. We would have practices, games, study hall—everything I needed to become a better player and person.

The school was located on Pleasant Avenue, which wasn't too far from my home. I knew it was a good move for me athletically and academically. Everyone knew I loved basketball, and that school would be a great place for me to get better and start building my name and my career.

I immediately went home and talked with my parents. They had always wanted the best for me, and so they did some research to find out how much the school would cost. The verdict was in: they couldn't afford it. There were a lot of things that had to be paid beforehand, such as the tuition fee, which was $200 per month. The school uniform was about $70, and gym clothes were another $50. My parents simply could not afford those expenses.

Dad got in touch with the coach of the school, Coach Mary Hallinan. She wanted to meet with my father to discuss whether I could attend Mt. Carmel Holy Rosary. However, she needed to see if I was worth it first and wanted to assess my skills and abilities. She had a practice session scheduled for later that day, so she conveniently invited us over.

At the practice session I introduced myself to Coach Mary, who was very kind and made me feel comfortable. "Ready to show me what you can do?" she asked me. Game on. She put me up against her best players. I had to go head to head with her lead point guard. It was too easy. I was quick and swift. I crossed over the players, shot three-pointers and drove to the basket. The coach was impressed with my talent.

I was the smallest player, but I had a big heart. Even at ten years old, I was able to do a lot of basketball tricks that a girl my age normally couldn't do. Crowds were stunned at how well I could handle the ball under pressure.

It was a great experience for me. I was confident and played my best to prove to the coach that I was serious about what I was doing. All I needed was a chance. I met with Coach Mary after practice ended, and she agreed to help me with the process of attending the school. All we really had to figure out was how my parents would pay the tuition every month.

Coach Mary put me through another test after that. She called over one of the boys from the boys' team. It was more of a challenge now. He was one of their top players, a starter for sure. I gave him a run for his money—the best challenge he got from a girl. He was a little over six feet tall, and I was only four feet, ten inches. He would post me up every chance he got, and while I was determined to win, he beat me.

Afterward, the point guard and the girls from the team complimented me. I was satisfied with my performance, because I gave it my all. After the meeting, Coach Mary said it was a go for me to attend the school; she would make sure the tuition fees were handled.

I went home excited. My parents were extremely proud of me. That day on the court, my journey started.

I waited and waited, and finally my parents told me that they had worked it out and that I would start classes in January 1997. I had the biggest smile on my face when I heard the news, because I knew I was making progress and getting one step closer to my dream to play in the WNBA.

I started my first day as a fifth-grader at the school. Nervous yet excited, I had to once again adjust to the new teachers and classmates, and this time coaches and teammates as well. I was worried about balancing classes and practices. This was my first time being on an organized team, so I wanted everyone to like and accept me.

My first day in class went well. I was quiet and very observant, speaking to everyone just to get a gauge on people. They were all nice and helpful, so I relaxed. It was a small school with a total of about five hundred students. There was no room for error.

Luckily, the school was within walking distance of my home. I could either walk or take the bus, which would drop me off in front of the school building. I mostly took the bus on cold or rainy days, but on days when the weather was nice, I enjoyed walking with classmates and talking with them on the way home.

When I finally settled in and became familiar with everyone, I prayed I didn't have to move to another school. I knew graduating was a goal I wanted to accomplish, so I had to stay focused. We had months of team practice and basketball lessons, along with after-school academic tutoring sessions and travel for games.

I'd never had this type of packed schedule, so it was new for me. Usually, I'd do everything on my own, and I was always disciplined because of my parents. I knew what my priorities were in life, and after a couple of months, I was relieved to know that I was at Mt. Carmel for good. We took team pictures, had nice uniforms and sneakers—basically the whole package. This was definitely the right place for me. It motivated me to increase my basketball knowledge and forced me to want to do well in my classes so I could play. I was getting ready for the next level: high school.

Our team became very popular, because we were winning every game during the season. The organization and school were getting a lot of attention. As for me, no one really believed I was working hard to use basketball to get to another level. They thought I only practiced and played for fun.

The summer before sixth grade, I spent a considerable amount of time working on my game, well into the night. I missed curfew and risked getting into trouble with my parents and making them worry. Still, I kept at it. All kinds of tough things happened in the projects I lived in—fights, shootings, robberies, and kidnappings—so my parents wanted me to be in the house before dark. When the time came for me to head inside, I would get mad and scream up to the window, asking if I could stay out a little longer. Sometimes my parents said yes, and sometimes no. Every opportunity I got, I was outside, working to sharpen my game with dribbling moves, layups, floaters, and jump shots.

I played in several local tournaments such as Kingdome and Showboat. Soon, I was known throughout New York City. I wanted to be well known, recognized, and remembered. No matter what, or where, or who I played against, I wanted to be known as a winner. That has never changed.

Summer tournaments were the best! Not having to worry about schoolwork allowed me to enjoy and fill every minute with basketball and have a great summer. When classes started again, it was back to business. With a tight schedule, I became robotic. My body and internal clock were trained so much that I didn't need my parents to wake me up at 6:00 a.m. for school. In fact, I sometimes woke them up. Classes, after-school practices, and tutoring became my life. I was so busy, I barely had time to eat dinner or shower when I got home.

I can honestly say I felt like a professional already. I didn't have time for anyone or anything except my business and basketball. I was on a professional schedule at an early age. I really didn't have much fun at that time, but that was by choice. Basketball and the school year forced me into a strict and good routine.

We won every game my sixth grade year. Sometimes I took over the games, scoring fifteen points or more, but I didn't need to. I had good players around me who knew what they were doing. With the energy I brought to every game, I started becoming popular. The year ended successfully, and I was looking forward to the seventh grade.

That summer was no different than the last one, and I spent it working hard. I awoke at 8:00 a.m. and shot hoops alone for about three hours. In the afternoon, I played one-on-one or three-on-three with mostly guys in a full-court game. It was tough playing with the guys. I got knocked down, my shots got blocked, and they posted me up a lot since I was so much shorter than them. Their competitiveness didn't stop me, though. I was always told to play to my strengths. I was a great defender, and I was getting stronger and sharper every day. Guys never expected the tricks I had up my sleeve to swipe the ball.

When I played with the girls, we won everywhere we went: West 4th, Milbank, Rod Strickland, and Rucker Park tournament. I even won MVP one year at Rucker. I was well known now, and my confidence soared. I was tough and ready to face anyone. People even gave me nicknames, the ultimate compliment, such as "Something Special," "She-Devil," "Don't Do It," and "Wizard of Oz."

During the seventh grade, I could feel myself growing as a person and getting wiser. The physical growth spurt, however, never arrived. One of my favorite teachers was Ms. Seltun. She showed how much she cared for me outside of basketball. We had conversations about life, the world, and every topic that came to mind. She was like a parent to me and influenced me to become a more mature person and a better player.

My mind was set to stay focused. It didn't mean I couldn't have fun; I just didn't want to do much of anything that didn't involve basketball. I told myself, "Business now, pleasure later." Growing up in Harlem, it was easy to get pulled into doing the wrong things or associating with the wrong people. I knew that one minor mistake could change my life for the worst. I had great parents and good people around me. I wanted to do things for my family. I didn't want us to struggle. I didn't have much, because it took my parents a long time to get on their feet, but I kept my head up and walked proud. A majority of the kids from the community and school wore name-brand clothes and sneakers, while I was simple in the way I dressed. We just didn't have the money for expensive clothes and shoes. I knew, however, I could be successful with hard work. What we endured was enough for me to know what a good, decent life was all about, and I wanted that security.

I promised myself I would make it big and not give up in life, no matter what the situation demanded.

There were tons of distractions and temptations in my neighborhood, and dealing with boys would be one of them. They came around often and attempted to tell me anything I wanted to hear just to get what they wanted. It was hard, but I didn't let anything or anyone get to me. I figured that was the way things had to be in order for me to reach my dreams.

When seventh grade ended, I found out that high school coaches would be at the summer tournaments to scout players they wanted to recruit to their schools. Temperatures rose to between 98 and 110 degrees, but I didn't care. I was dedicated to my game.

I ended up at the hospital once on a summer day in August. The weather was intolerable that evening, but still, I decided to go outside and play basketball in the rain. I was always told different things about what great players did in order to become successful. So, dedicating myself to being the best, I took everyone's advice, and decided to practice in the rain. My chest began getting sore and the exertion made it worse. I eventually ended up being admitted to the hospital because of fluid around my heart, a condition called Pericarditis. The doctors also found a small murmur in my heart, which was slightly alarming. After a few days of rest, I was good to go. When I got better, I started working out again. It was scary at first, but I pressed on.

Summer was over and school was back in session. After tryouts Coach Mary put me on the team right away, and I was given a scholarship to play for the school for another year. We began playing other schools and doing well, so Coach Mary decided to put me in the starting lineup.

I was happy with how I was living, and I was enjoying basketball so much that it became my leisure time as well as my craft. I didn't have any interest in anything else but basketball. It was really nice playing with my teammates, even though some of my teammates were a little distant and not so friendly.

We played at Riverbank State Park in a Queen Latifah tournament, where I did really well in all aspects of the game—three-pointers, layups, assists, and jump shots. I had the fans jumping up and down with excitement.

The school year was fun, but I was ready for the 1997 summer tournaments. By now, my name had circulated throughout the New York City basketball community, and the boys wanted to outplay me. I was ready for anyone who stepped on the court, and I embarrassed a lot of boys playing ball. They brought the challenge, and I loved it.

The boys began to respect me and stopped doubting my game just because I was short, young, and a girl. The team I started out with was no longer together, so I joined an all-girls team to finish the summer tournaments. I helped bring the team a championship and received several trophies for MVP, best athlete, and sportsmanship. Summer was drawing to a close, and the start of school was near.

I was ready for a new year in school, but basketball was still my priority.

It was tough for me to adjust in Catholic school because I had to wear a dress or skirt. That didn't go well with playing basketball, but it didn't stop me. We were struggling, because my dad couldn't work, and that left us in a financial need. I went to school at times in the winter when it was freezing outside with only a skirt on, no tights or leg warmers, and even though I was freezing, I played basketball in the same shoes until the heel of the shoe was practically gone. That didn't bother me. I don't know if the kids ever made fun of me, but if they did, it didn't matter.

I can recall a time when Mt. Carmel had a double-header game against another school. The girls played first. It was a challenging game, but the victory was ours because we were all involved in the game, playing as a team. Once the game with the girls ended, the boys began to play. As the game reached halftime, our boys were losing.

The coach said, "Shannon, get dressed!"

I thought he was joking, but he wasn't. I put on my uniform and got into the game. I immediately made an impact and brought energy to the team. We began to score and close the lead. Before the last quarter, we took the lead and won. I will never forget that moment. Coach Dyson, the coach for the boys' team, was extremely happy. It made me feel so good to know I could help him get a victory.

As great as I was on the court, during middle school I often struggled in the classroom. It was the one period in my life in which I didn't study much. My grades weren't looking good, so my parents began to help me with my class work so I could catch up. It was then that I realized how important my education was, and I began to pay more attention in class in order to fulfill my long-term goal of graduating and playing in the WNBA. The school season went well and summer rolled around, which meant it was time to start up summer tournaments.

In the summer of 1998, I was introduced to a new coach who went by the name "Hammer." He was the coach for a recreational center called The Children's Aid Society. The team, the Douglas Panthers, was a girls' team. I met new friends, and it was fun. We got along and played well together. We played in summer tournaments all over New York City.

I especially remember a game at Roberto Clemente State Park. I was shooting three-pointers, driving to the basket, and scoring layups. It was fun playing with new teammates and hearing the fans enjoying the game. Every game was an adrenaline rush for me.

I always felt a little nervous at first because I wasn't used to the crowd, but after a few minutes up and down the court, I let loose and ran the floor like a champion. When it came to girls' basketball, the Douglas Panthers began to make a name for ourselves in New York. We were playing in different tournaments and in gyms where pro basketball players had played, such as Rucker Park and Gauchos Gym.

During one game at Gauchos, a boy was told to try and take the ball from me. He tried hard to take the ball, and I had him spinning in circles trying to get it, but he couldn't get it away from me. Everyone was laughing, entertained. My handle was natural. I never practiced handling the ball the way I do; it's always been a blessing to me.

When I entered the eighth grade in September 1999, I knew it was time to pour my heart into my last year at Mt. Carmel so that I could attend a good high school. I was taught about the importance of school and was told over and over again, "No school, no ball." I listened to the people that had my best interests at heart, and my parents played the biggest role in that motivation.

Eighth grade was very demanding, and the work became increasingly more difficult. This grew to be an issue for me. I had to make sure I passed my exams and qualified for the high schools I wanted to attend. I had my eye on schools with good academics and good basketball teams, such as Cardinal Spellman, St. Raymond's, Monsignor Scanlan, Bishop Loughlin, and Manhattan Center.

I focused hard on passing my exams. I stayed late after school with teachers for tutoring and did whatever it took to make sure that I would graduate. In the meantime, I maintained my golden touch as a player, and our team became a powerhouse. Mt. Carmel started getting so much recognition that a lot of aspiring middle-school athletes wanted to attend the school. I knew I had contributed to that, and it made me feel great. Even though my time as an athlete was showing great results, it was still hard to shake off the worry of whether or not I would pass my school exams. After all, those scores would determine whether I would graduate middle school or get held back.

A month before graduation day, the teachers finally let the students know their results. The students who passed were told to show up for graduation rehearsal. When I was told I had to join rehearsal, I was so happy I felt like flying. I didn't even ask questions about the rehearsals; I just wanted to graduate and head to high school.

We finished as champs at Mt. Carmel, and graduation rehearsals took a couple of weeks. We practiced what to sing and how to walk. We were ready to make our families proud of us. Classes were done, games were over, and all that was left were the goodbyes and the "see you in the future" conversations.

On graduation day, everyone was ecstatic. Cameras clicked and bright light flashes blinded us as family members took countless photographs. I'd say we, as students, were the most excited about getting our diplomas. When it was my turn, I walked up on stage proudly, looking out at the audience. As I walked off with my diploma in hand, I felt a sense of relief. My middle school years were complete.

After the summer ended a new year began, and I repeated my routine of playing ball and going to school. By then my real motive for going to school was to play basketball in the WNBA.

One summer, I participated in a clinic that took place at the Martin Luther King Jr. Towers, just west of Harlem. Buildings fifteen stories high surrounded me. A place like that was described as "the projects," and it was no place for safety. Basketball was my life and I wasn't going to let anything get in the way of that, not even the fear of my own safety.

During middle and high school summers at home, I would wake up at nine every morning and shoot hoops outside alone until others came to join me. I'd end up playing the entire day and wouldn't go upstairs until 9:00 p.m., my curfew.

When I was thirteen years old, Rucker Park hosted the famous Entertainers Basketball Classic (EBC) tournament, and I wanted to see who was playing there. The tournament promoted education, and your grades determined whether you could play.

It was a remarkable event. The park seated hundreds of people, and several celebrities came to watch and play as well. Games there were aired on television and on the Internet. It was no wonder; Rucker Park was a very popular court, and its reputation preceded it. The most legendary players in history played there—Kareem Abdul-Jabbar and Julius Erving played against New York City's best street ballers, such as Joe Hammond, aka "The Destroyer." The park gained recognition across the country because of these prominent players and their memorable experiences.

Although the court was legendary, a hostile environment lurked within. It was always packed, and the spectators were tough to please; it was much worse than any of the crowds that I had seen or played in front of. Not only was the crowd intimidating, but they were literally close enough to touch you while you were on the court. If you ever got the chance to play in this park tournament, though, it was a confirmation of your talent.

The tournament usually started around 6:00 p.m., just after sundown. The announcer entertained the crowd, and they often held dancing competitions or had live performances during halftime. People from the crowd were often chosen to participate, and the music was loud enough for people staying home to hear and enjoy.

The celebrity who showed up the day I attended the tournament was NBA player Rafer Alston, also known as "Skip to My Lou." Since he was one of my favorite players, I was naturally excited when he put on a show. I wish I'd had my camera then, because that was a moment I wanted to capture forever. I returned to the park again when I heard another celebrity, NBA player Allen Iverson, was coming to play. However, he didn't arrive, so at halftime, the organizers needed some entertainment to fill the gap. They called for two people from the crowd to come to the court and play against each other.

My friends suggested I go and show my talent, but I was extremely nervous. If you didn't bring your game at Rucker Park, you were put to shame. Nevertheless, I went onto the court to play against the boy who had volunteered. We were the same age and even had the same first name. He was only a few inches taller than I was.

The crowd cheered for both of us, excited about the matchup. The boy Shannon displayed all the moves he had, trying to cross me over and even make me fall. But his moves weren't good enough—not for me, at least. He went for a layup but missed the shot, and then it was my turn. I started dribbling the ball, and the crowd's cheers got louder and louder. I could see I was intimidating the boy by the way I was handling the basketball.

I drove to the basket with a layup and scored. The spectators jumped out of their seats, and people were throwing money at me on the court. I didn't know what to do—the roar of the crowd was deafening. People were hanging onto the fence surrounding the park, shouting names at me like "Lil Bit" and "Something Special." Who knows? Maybe I was something special.

Rucker Park appreciated my skill on the court, and from that day on, I became popular. I was invited to do a shoot for a website called HoopsTV.com. I accepted because I wanted to do all I could to get the exposure and make it to the WNBA. I went down to West 4th Street to do the video shoot. They put me in a game with some ballers who were already there, and I played while being recorded. After the game, the other players were asked about my performance, and everyone gave positive comments, stating I had the potential to go pro.

We traveled to different sites to film. We went to Brooklyn to do a video for Dunk.net, and I went up against men. There was one guy who wanted the ball; he had doubts about my game. I was only thirteen, but I was tough. This guy was playing me close and getting frustrated because he couldn't take the ball.

He hounded me closely, so I began doing all types of handles with the ball to see if he could take it. He couldn't. I drove to the basket, and just as I did, he stuck his shoulder out and knocked me down. Everyone jumped up, disapproving of the way I was sent to the ground. I jumped up, got the ball and came at him again. I got by him with tight handles, shifting the basketball between my legs, his legs, and the legs of every defender that came at me. I drove to the basket and scored.

After the game, spectators commented about the game and my performance. Everyone was mentioning the WNBA. Some were saying WNBA for sure. It gave me a good feeling; I felt truly blessed.

I also ended up being featured in a documentary called *Ball Above All*, and I was the only female in it. I played against guys in a tournament that took place in a park in lower Manhattan, and passersby stopped to watch once they realized it was a girl playing against bigger, stronger guys. Soon everyone who saw me mentioned the documentary. It was a great experience that prepared me for professional life. I was blessed to have the opportunity to be on websites, DVDs, and television at a young age, and while at the time I didn't know where this would take me, it brought me a long way.

After doing videos for these websites, I was offered a chance to do a WNBA Father's Day commercial. That was something I was really excited about. A car was sent to our home to take my parents and me to New Jersey, and once we arrived, the director explained that he wanted me to play against someone who would pretend to be my father in the commercial. My fake dad and I got to know each other and messed around with the ball a bit before beginning the official shoot.

The commercial went like this:

I was outside shooting around in the driveway when "Dad" came up and said, "Hey Shannon, would you like to shoot a game of hoops with Dad?" I accepted the offer, and they filmed me from different angles and positions as I began crossing him over and spinning around him as he turned in circles. It was a humorous commercial, and in it I won the game. Filming took most of the day, from 7:00 a.m. to 5:00 p.m. I was tired, but I couldn't wait for the commercial to air on television. When Father's Day came around, the WNBA game was on and I saw the commercial. Everyone was happy for me. I received phone calls from friends and family telling me they saw me on television. It was a feeling that I will never forget.

After the commercial aired, ESPN asked for a magazine and video interview, and we accepted. They came to our apartment to talk to me and to film the trophies I had earned in tournaments over the years. Once the magazine issue was published, I was given a few copies, and it made me very proud. The people in my community respected me for being a positive influence on other kids. Basketball was very popular in our housing project, and I was being a good role model. I realized that whatever I was doing, I had to keep doing it because it must be right.

As for the summer, I had basketball to focus on again. Every year in late June, a big tournament called Kingdome took place practically outside of my apartment window. The crowd was enormous, and you could feel its force as fans cheered on the players, all of whom put on magnificent performances. I always tried to be present at every game.

When I got my chance to play on the Kingdome Court, I amused the crowd with my handle, taking it to some of the popular male players who were up to the challenge. At times the crowd roared at such a volume that my parents would run to the window, thinking something bad had happened. As time went on, I found myself getting treated like a celebrity.

I was a big fan of WNBA star Cynthia Cooper and Tennessee Coach Pat Summitt. I wanted to get to know them both and play for Summitt and the Lady Volunteers. Cynthia Cooper was embarking on her fourth championship with the Houston Comets at that time, and I actually got a chance to meet her just before a game in 2000, when she came to New York to play the Liberty. She'd heard about me and was willing to give me a moment of her time to talk about my talent and potential. She was very lovely and kind, and she gave me confidence. I was concerned about my size, because I was told my height would hold me back on a professional level. Cooper told me to perfect my game, work on getting to the basket, and just believe in myself. She even watched some of the videos of me playing and commented that she liked the moves that I had, such as dribbling the ball behind my back and bringing it back with only one hand.

At the end of our meeting, I wished her well in her championship game. They won and she received her fourth MVP award and her fourth WNBA championship ring. Cooper's words stayed with me and helped me to deal with the doubts of other people for years to come.

## 3. THE MIRROR

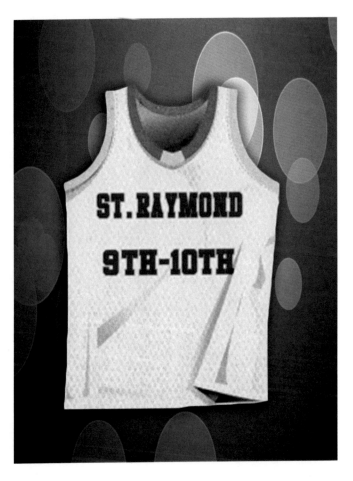

I had no idea where I would end up for high school.
Around August, letters came in from all the schools
I was interested in attending. I wasn't sure which

school to pick, but after some thought, I chose a Catholic school in the Bronx called St. Raymond's Academy for Girls. I was told that St. Raymond's was a good school academically but that it didn't have a good basketball team. I felt I could make a difference for the team, so I decided to attend.

Traveling to St. Raymond's was a journey in and of itself because of the distance. My commute was filled with bus and train transfers, which made me nervous in the beginning, because I had never traveled alone on public transportation up until that point. I am naturally an early bird, so I'd wake up at 5:00 a.m., take a shower, and then take the bus to the train, which was always packed in the morning. It was very uncomfortable at times. The train ride to my destination was about twelve stops. After getting off of the train, I had to walk another half mile just to get to the school.

A typical day at St. Raymond's wasn't much different from my schedule in middle school. I arrived at school by 8:00 a.m. and classes ended by

2:30 p.m. I was a shy student, and I didn't say much in class because I wasn't sure if my answers would be correct. So, I thought it was best just to listen and take notes. If I had any questions, I always waited until class was over to speak to the teacher in private.

After classes, I usually did homework until it was time for practice or a game. Practices typically lasted two hours or so, depending on whether the team needed additional work. By the time I got home it was 8:00 or 9:00 p.m., and I was exhausted. I didn't have time to study or even tell my family how the day went; I just ate, showered, and went to bed early. My schedule stayed the same from elementary school all the way through high school. That schedule worked best for me; it helped me stay organized and do well.

Playing in high school was very demanding. I had to make sure my grades were good in order to stay on the team. I struggled often since I wasn't the brightest student. I had to work hard to make sure I passed my classes.

Unfortunately for me, our team didn't win many games, and I wasn't getting much exposure. The school wasn't known yet for its girls' basketball team. I wasn't invited to many summer basketball camps, so that showed me I had to work harder to be recognized. Only girls who were exceptionally talented were invited to such camps.

I played at St. Raymond's for two years until I decided I should move to a school that was more competitive. I transferred to Murry Bergtraum High School in 2003, which was my junior year. My father met with Coach Ed Grezinsky, who stated that I would be a good addition to the team. This time my parents didn't have to pay for anything, because Murry Bergtraum was a public school. It was ultimately a good decision for me because the school fared well academically and athletically.

# 4. A DRAWING WORTH 1,000 WORDS

When I arrived at Murry Bergtraum, the basketball team was already a winning program; I just had to help continue the winning tradition. Because of my work ethic and will to win, I fit in well with my teammates. I knew I would become a better player at this school and have a good opportunity to get into a good college, as well. My fate was where I wanted it to be—in my hands.

As for our team, we had to deal with some stiff competition, meaning we had to make sure we played our best in every game. The strong teams we had to face included the Manhattan Center, Frederick Douglass, and Francis Lewis, to name a few. I played in the backcourt with another future WNBA player, Epiphanny Prince. We were two exciting guards to watch, and we were determined and firm in our goal to be the best. We worked together and won many games.

Our team went on to play in the state championship game my junior year. We played against Christ the King High School, which was the best private school in Queens, New York. Their players were clever and very tall, and they had the best post player in the tristate area at the time, Tina Charles. As seasoned players who refused to give up during any game, we played hard and found a way to get the win. I was so excited; I was a champion. All I wanted to do was continue being victorious and become a great point guard. I was told that people only remember winners, and that was what I would be.

When the new basketball season started in November, I noticed that my teammates weren't involving me much in the games. They hardly passed me the ball, and I felt excluded. I didn't know what had happened, but I tried to ignore it and stay focused.

All I cared about was contributing to the team's victories. I didn't really care about the special awards; I was content with myself as a player. Some players only care about themselves or their individual achievements—not what they can accomplish together as one team. In our case, this egotism cost us games, because no one respected or trusted each other. Basketball is a physical team sport; you need great chemistry in order to do well, which was something we didn't have at this point. This was a tremendous problem, especially for me as the point guard.

The point guard is an extension of the coach—the one who sets the tempo of the game—so we have one of the most important jobs on the court. Point guards are equivalent to quarterbacks in American football. Their job is to make sure their teammates are placed in areas where they'll be able to score easily.

Point guards are triple-threat players, meaning they must be able to shoot, dribble, and pass the ball. My forte was dribbling. As a point guard I was supposed to make the other players' jobs easier, but I couldn't do that if my team neglected to pass me the ball and wouldn't work together. When things go wrong in a game, point guards get the blame. When things go right, they get the credit. So the fact that our team couldn't get along weighed heavily on me.

We didn't do too well at the start of the season, but we gradually improved. We tackled our problems by discussing what everyone's goals were and what issues we had with one another. After talking, we realized that winning a championship was the most important thing to each of us, and it would help all of our futures if we were able to win again.

My teammates believed in me, and in return I believed in them. Understanding and believing in one another enabled us to play well together. We were on all of the sports pages as one of the city's top contenders, and we made our way into the playoffs. We constantly faced tough competition, but my teammates and I worked hard and made it to the city championship game again, this year held at Madison Square Garden. To me, it was the closest thing to being a professional at the time. The game was televised, which meant my friends and family could watch me play on TV.

Right before a game, my normal routine was to listen to relaxing music as well as some hype music. I prayed for an injury-free game, for me to play well, and of course, for us to win. I stretched and went on the court a little early to get familiar with the rims, the court itself, and the basketball. Thirty minutes before tipoff, the players were in the locker room listening to the game plan from the coach and getting ready to warm up as a team. I was so nervous because all of my family and friends would be watching, and everyone had high expectations of me to do well and to win.

I felt that pressure as we warmed up with layups and shooting drills. I could hear people in the stands yelling my name, and I tried my best to stay focused on my teammates and the game plan instead of worrying about the fans, the crowd, or the opponents warming up on the other side of the court. With the clock winding down to tipoff time, I was feeling increasingly more nervous about the game, because I had no idea how I would play. I had confidence in my team, but when it's the championship game and two great teams are competing, you never know what could happen.

The horn finally went off, and it was time to announce each team's starting lineup. We were all talking to each other, making sure we were ready to compete and win the city title at Madison Square Garden. I could see in everyone's eyes that they were nervous, but I also knew we had prepared well and had a great shot at winning the game. My name was called, and the crowd cheered so loudly that I felt at home. Now, I was ready to play. The game started, and we never looked back. We played hard, got defensive stops, and scored every chance we could to make sure we secured a win.

That's just what we did. We won the title, and I was ecstatic. I put on my championship shirt and hat and ran all around the court. It was a highlight of my high school career, and I couldn't have been any happier than I was in that moment. We all were laughing, joking, and dancing; it was a moment to remember. We received our team trophy, took pictures, and participated in many media interviews expressing what the victory meant to the school and for our careers. I was blessed to be a part of a successful program, and I was happy I was able to contribute to a win for the school.

After the game was over, I greeted my family with hugs and kisses and said hello to all of my friends and fans that had come to support me. Then I went home and hung out in my housing project after the game like it was a normal day. I would never forget where I came from, and I enjoyed spending time with my friends in the housing project.

Still, school and basketball were not yet over, so I had to make sure my academic priorities were in order while preparing with my teammates for the state tournament. We knew that title game would be a tough match as well.

The day of the match, as the game got started, I charged forward, feeling confident in my team. We were getting cheered, and I could practically feel the crowd's excitement. It sent chills up my spine and gave me the extra energy to keep going. The game was good, but by no means easy. We scored, our opponent scored, and this continued back and forth until the Murry Bergtraum Lady Blazers took over the game.

I attacked the basket, got layups, made a few steals on defense, and set my teammates up to score. We won the game and became the 2003 city and state champions. We celebrated joyfully, and I felt like my plan to make it to the WNBA was falling into place. Everything I did was credited to determination. Transferring to a great school, being part of a wonderful team, and winning the state championship made my junior year an absolutely amazing journey.

The summer before my senior year, summer tournaments were cranking up again. I was asked to play in a tournament with Exodus in Baltimore, Maryland, which was about a three-hour trip from

New York City. I asked the coach to talk to my father because I had never traveled that far to play.

The coach assured my father that he would take care of me and ensure my safety. He also said he was putting us in a five-star hotel, so my dad agreed to let me go. We traveled in a fifteen-passenger van, which wasn't in the best condition. I was so uncomfortable—I couldn't wait to get there. We finally made it to Maryland, but were met with disappointment. Our hotel was not a five-star, nor a four, or even a three-star establishment. My parents decided to meet us there to attend the games, and it was a good thing they did. When they arrived, they noticed the hotel conditions. The van wouldn't start the next morning, and the ignition was spinning around, clearly broken.

My dad decided that was enough. He told the coach he was taking me home, and we went back to New York. It had been an unpleasant trip to Maryland, but I was back in the city, back home, and ready for my senior year.

However, my last year of high school proved to be quite difficult. I wanted to make sure I graduated. I was focused on passing my classes and prepping for the SAT and ACT college entrance exams. My grades weren't great, but I was passing; I needed to get high SAT and ACT scores. I knew it would be challenging for me, but I tried my hardest, hoping I'd get lucky and be able to go to a Division I school. If not, I'd have to go to junior college for two years before transferring to a Division I school.

The first time I took the SAT, I didn't get a high enough score. So I studied for a couple of months and took the test again. This time, I knew I did well. I felt I had the right answers, but when the test results came, I missed the mark by one point. I ended up taking both the SAT and the ACT exam at least four times each. It was incredibly annoying and stressful, since both of the tests lasted about four hours. I wasn't the best student in school, so naturally, I wasn't much of a test-taker.

I never got the score I wanted on those exams, and this saddened me so much that I wanted to give up. I thought going to a junior college would be my downfall and that people would forget about me. I felt like it wasn't a great career move. In desperation, I even thought about going to prep school; at least that way I would be able to have all four years of eligibility at a Division I basketball program. My parents didn't like that idea too much. I started thinking that my chances of getting to the WNBA were slim.

By this point, I was extremely stressed. In addition to not getting the SAT/ACT scores I wanted, I began failing my exams. Basketball practices felt harder, more rigorous, and longer. The games were more challenging. I couldn't score and committed too many turnovers. Nothing seemed to be going right.

Near the end of the basketball season, we were able to pick up our game. We began doing well, blowing out teams throughout the city. As we approached the 2004 championship, I could feel a lot of weight on my shoulders. Getting good grades was one of the hardest struggles I have ever faced. I was the only player on my team that didn't qualify for a Division I scholarship.

Ironically, this was the period when I grew the most as a person and student. I had to tell myself that I had come too far to give up; I had a goal and a dream that needed to be completed. I had to work harder in my classes and continue to learn from my mistakes on the court so I could qualify for a scholarship to college. Some of the mistakes I made in my classes happened because I was not asking the teachers for more help. I was too embarrassed to admit I didn't understand the work. This hurt me in the long run, because when I had to take the exams, I didn't know the material well enough to get good grades.

The mistakes on the court were fewer because I worked really hard. I could always improve my weaknesses, and I did so every year. As a point guard with the ball in your hands the majority of the time, you are bound to make mistakes. The game of basketball is an instinctive sport with little time to think. You take what your opponents give you, and you react to their reactions to you. I learned from every turnover I made and every loss we suffered.

This struggle on and off the court made me the person I am today. My work ethic and determination helped me to strive for the best in life, despite not being such a good student in school. I made sure I had my priorities in order.

My parents did a great job raising me; I was well rounded and knew what was most important. As a result, my dating life was very limited. My dad was disciplined and tough, yet very loving and caring toward his kids. Although I wasn't allowed to have a boyfriend until I was eighteen years old, I was a curious little girl growing up. I always showed my liking for a boy by flirting with him or staring at him, but I knew I could not take it any further than that. I wasn't allowed to have boys call my home or visit. If I had any interest in a boy, I had to spend time with him during school, but even that was hard, because I had to focus on school. So I snuck around after school to see the boys I was talking to.

Some guys I dated were street guys who weren't going to school. They always had money and lived the "fast life." I could have easily chosen that path that promised fast money, because it was all around me and offered to me from the guys I secretly dated. But with the supportive cast in my corner, I was always told to stay focused and leave the boys alone, because the consequences would not be worth the fast life and dealing with guys who weren't about positivity. I could have gotten pregnant at an early age or arrested for being in the wrong place at the wrong time. A lot would have been different if I had not had a strong mind to stay focused on school and basketball. Distractions were everywhere, and everywhere I went, I had temptations. Not to mention, I made some bad decisions at times by leaving school early to go spend time with boys that didn't have a positive future. Anything could have happened, but God definitely protected me during those dangerous and reckless times in my life.

We won the city championship again at Madison Square Garden. I had to push away all of the stress and clear my head in order to play well. We played against Christ the King High School in Glens Falls, a great team and the number one Catholic program. With a great crowd and a competitive game, I worked hard with my teammates to help bring us closer to victory. I hustled up and down the court and fired terrific passes that made the crowd whistle, cheer, and shout. I could see kids in the stands having a great time, and that made me feel good. It was a feeling of accomplishment. I loved the competition; it brought out the best in me and made me forget about everything for a while.

We won the 2004 championship game, making us state champions for the second year in a row. It is always hard to repeat, so it was a big deal for the program and the players. We all had huge smiles on our faces, hugged each other, and shed tears of joy. We showed a lot of determination and resilience, and our hard work paid off when it counted. I received a lot of calls, text messages, and emails when I checked my phone after the game. I tried to enjoy the moment now that my basketball mission was over in high school. To celebrate the victory, I went out to eat, and spend time with family and friends.

School was still in session, so I had to stay focused. I was proud of the team and myself. Still, I was worried about finishing my senior year and wondered whether I would get into a Division I college of my choice. It was too late to take the ACT or SAT again. I didn't get an offer from any university, and I became worried and unsure of what to do, so I asked Coach Grezinsky. He suggested that I attend a good community college and take the long route. Apprehensively, I took his advice. I finished out the school year, but when graduation day came, I didn't attend. Instead, I played basketball. Several community colleges were willing to take me, but I wanted to be on a top-notch and competitive team.

Despite my worries, I was happy with my accomplishments at Murry Bergtraum. We had done exactly what I wanted to do when I decided to attend the school: we won back-to-back championships.

# 5. DOUBLE ZERO

Coach Grezinsky, or Coach G, as we called him, helped me make my final college decision. I chose Trinity Valley Community College, a two-year college in Athens, Texas. In order to get a head start on everything and familiarize myself with my new home and team, I decided to take summer classes there. It was 2004, I was only eighteen years old, and leaving home to be on my own for the very first time was a frightening feeling.

I made the trip to Texas by plane, which was only my second time flying. When I arrived, I was nervous and didn't know what to expect. I would be living with my new coach, Michael Landers, and his wife during the summer until the fall semester began, and all I could do was trust that I was in good hands with him. Coach Landers assured me that he would help me get acclimated to the campus, and to Athens, until I could get around on my own.

Although Athens was only an hour and a half away from the city of Dallas, it was a completely different town than what I was used to in New York. Yet this was a place I had to get comfortable with, as it was going to be my home for two years. There was little change in the weather; the sun shone brightly, and it was hot every single day. The town consisted mostly of grocery stores and fast-food restaurants. Trinity Valley's college campus was small, so there was never much to do. The town was all country, so for a girl like me, who had grown up in the city that never sleeps with something to do every minute, it was difficult to adjust.

On the other hand, living with Coach Landers and his wife was pleasant. They treated me well and made me feel welcome in their home. Since the fall semester had not yet begun, a lot of my Lady Cardinal teammates weren't on campus yet, so I hadn't met them. Still, I practiced individually.

Soon, I felt like I had gotten accustomed to living away from home, but then I started getting homesick. I missed my family a lot and always felt like returning home. I kept in constant touch with my family, and that helped me deal with it.

When the fall semester began, I moved into a dorm room on campus. I didn't have a roommate for the first year, but I didn't mind. Classes started, and the Lady Cardinals began practicing as a team. I learned quickly that I couldn't play street ball at the collegiate level. I had to learn plays and remember them. We were given a lot of different plays for defense and offense, as well as for baseline and sideline out-of-bounds. It was overwhelming at times. I modeled my game after great point guards like John Stockton and Mark Jackson. I worked on getting the ball to the scorers and aimed to set the tempo of the game. I learned when to use my street savvy talents, and when necessary, I impacted the game with my scoring ability. Sometimes I was able to take over games without even scoring.

Things went well, I made new friends, and the chemistry I shared with the team was great. I found my comfort zone and focused on the future; I had to make the best of my junior college years in order to make it to the University of Tennessee, a college I had dreamed of attending since I was a little girl.

Coach Landers liked my game right away. As the season began, I was relaxed and felt in control on the court. I played freely with no restrictions, just running the floor and scoring, bringing the full package and experience I'd gotten from my years of playing basketball in New York City. The team did well, so we were all happy. Things looked good for us, even though we weren't considered a big threat. By this point, the bouts of homesickness had stopped. With new friends, an awesome team, and good classes, I had nothing to worry about.

After my first college year in 2004-05 at Trinity Valley, I realized my grades weren't anything to brag about to anyone. A bit disappointed, I decided to stay on campus that summer to study. I had a goal and would do whatever was needed to accomplish it. I studied vigorously the whole summer, with very few breaks to mingle with friends.

When my second and final year at Trinity Valley began, I was ready to face it. I wanted to be successful so that I could graduate and attend the university I wanted. One of my teammates decided to live with me, so I finally had a roommate. Busy with classes, tutoring, team practices, and games, I didn't have any idea how stressed I was until that first night of the semester.

I was asleep in my dorm room when I suddenly jerked awake, unable to breathe, not sure if it had been a bad dream. My chest tightened until I was gasping for air. I panicked, feeling nervous and scared. This had never happened to me before. My heart pounded so hard I thought it would burst out of my body. I couldn't reach out for help; it was past two in the morning, and the room was shrouded in darkness. I didn't want to disturb my roommate since she was sleeping, but I had to say something. I could hardly breathe and felt like this was going to be my last day alive.

I woke up my roommate and with some difficulty explained what was happening. She repeatedly told me to calm down and relax, comforting me as best as she could.

"Don't think about things you can't control," she said. "Just relax. Let's watch some TV."

She stayed up with me to try and distract me from my feelings and make me focus on something else. Eventually, I was able to calm down. My heart started to feel normal again. I drank a glass of water, and my roommate and I went back to sleep.

The next afternoon we had practice. After morning classes, I came early to the gym to speak privately to Coach Landers. I told him about my anxiety and what had happened overnight. Coach Landers suggested that I see a psychiatrist, and he set up an appointment for me for a couple of days later. However, I didn't want my teammates to see me talking to a psychiatrist. I didn't want them to think I was crazy, or sick, so I met with the psychiatrist right before practice; that way, our session would be private and confidential. We talked for a few hours.

He told me to let everything out and asked me different questions. When did these feelings come? What brought them on? I explained that the attacks came randomly. I'd start putting pressure on myself, thinking about things like life and death and how I never wanted to fail. With nothing to distract me, the attacks came, and I felt helpless.

The psychiatrist took notes and suggested a number of strategies that would help me cope and remember that the situation was created in my head. He suggested I take a brown paper bag and breathe into it if I had another episode. He made me feel better by saying I was completely healthy and reassuring me that nothing was wrong with me.

My conversations with him helped a lot, and I also educated myself about anxiety. I had to learn everything about it in order to figure out how to fix the problem. I learned that anxiety comes when the mind focuses on too many different things at the same time, causing stress and worry about getting everything done.

To me, the mind is like a computer. When a computer is on and you have too many windows open, the computer may run slower and may even eventually freeze. That's how my anxiety attack felt. I needed a way to keep myself from drowning in the worry. Over time, I came to understand why anxiety attacks happen and how to control any episodes.

With my anxiety issues under control, I was able to help my teammates play winning basketball. I was selected as the Junior College Player of the Year and was also selected to be a Junior College All-American in 2006.

My parents, sister, several of my brothers, and a cousin decided to attend one of my games in Texas before I graduated. They drove from New York City to attend, and came to watch me practice first. During that particular practice session, we had a surprise visit from a scout named Dean Lockwood, the assistant coach for the Tennessee Lady Volunteers, one of the top universities in the country for women's basketball. I couldn't believe it. He just sat there and smiled. Due to NCAA recruiting rules, Coach Lockwood was not permitted to speak to any players—but he could talk to our coach. (There are rules during different periods of the recruiting calendar when coaches who are recruiting are allowed to talk to players, and vice versa.) Although I wished I could speak with him, doing so would have been a violation of NCAA rules, and I didn't want to jeopardize my eligibility.

We had great practices at Trinity Valley every day, and we each improved individually and as a team. Several Division I coaches visited during recruiting periods to evaluate players they wanted to offer scholarships. We were one of the top junior colleges and had great players in different positions. I was excited to see Coach Lockwood, and I wanted to make sure I gave him a great first and last impression so he would see my skills and personality as a point guard.

With my parents there as well, I was especially driven to work hard to make them proud of me. It was interesting to see a big time coach come to watch a practice instead of a game, but doing so enabled them to witness your work ethic and what you did to get better away from game day attention. That day really motivated me to practice hard and always stay focused, because you never knew which college coach would walk through the doors and watch your practice.

I had watched Tennessee several times on television and said to myself, "I want to play there, and I know I can." The fans were great, the bright orange colors were very loud, and Pat Summitt was a legendary coach who everyone wanted to meet—and play for—when it came to college basketball. That day was special for me, and it opened my eyes to what my future could be once I finished junior college. C. Vivian Stringer of Rutgers was another coach from a top program who came to watch our practices. The season was going well for us, and we were projected to win a national title, but we fell short to Kansas.

Our last game of the season was in the state of Kansas. It was a conference tournament, but my game wasn't quite as sharp. I missed shots and had a couple of turnovers. It just wasn't me. Unfortunately, we lost. The buzzer sounded, signaling the end of the game. As I prepared to walk off the court, I had a feeling that someone was watching me. I happened to look over, and to my surprise, it was the coach of Tennessee, Pat Summitt—the same head coach that I had dreamed of playing for one day.

Shockingly to me, Coach Summitt was impressed with my performance even though I felt like I had played a lousy game. She said she liked the way I ran the floor. I never noticed her during the game; Summitt said it showed that I was focused.

After our last game, I focused on finishing classes and preparing for graduation. The tension was at its peak—I had to start visiting universities and choose the one I wanted to attend for the next two years. I was waiting to hear from a good university, but everything seemed to be moving slowly. No one got in touch with my coach right away. It was completely nerve-wracking. Coach Landers did tell me about several universities that wanted me, but those colleges weren't the ones I was interested in attending.

Then one day, Coach Landers came to me with good news from the University of Maryland and Rutgers University—two of the biggest colleges for women's basketball. Both were on top, academically and athletically, so I was excited to hear from them. My luck finally seemed to be changing. I spoke to Coach Brenda Frese, the head coach from the University of Maryland, to set up a visit and contacted my family and friends to tell them the good news.

We were prepared for the trip when Coach Frese contacted me again. I was hoping it would be good news, but it wasn't. Coach Frese informed me that she had picked up another point guard who had asked to transfer from Tennessee. There goes my chance, I thought. Upset, I called my family to give them the bad news. Then, I realized something: Tennessee didn't have a point guard now—which meant the Lady Vols were looking for one—which in turn meant I could fill that position! I finally had the opportunity to attend my dream university as the Lady Vols point guard!

Apparently, the Lady Vols felt the same way, because they asked me to visit their campus. I was shocked and in disbelief. I was nearly on my toes, so excited to tell everyone the good news.

Shortly after the Lady Vols' invitation, Coach Stringer contacted me with an invitation to visit the Rutgers campus. I decided to attend a Rutgers basketball game, where I spoke to some of the players and staff. The school seemed like a good choice because it was close to home and had a good basketball program, but I had to visit Tennessee before I made my final decision.

I met Coach Pat Summitt again during my visit to the University of Tennessee. She was very kind and had a great sense of humor. I was surprised, because on the court she was aggressive and demanding. It was an unexpected encounter. We had dinner together and talked about what my role would be on the team. She was frank and said I had to earn the starting position, so I did just that. I felt like I belonged at Tennessee—this was my place to be. It was an automatic feeling. My parents agreed with my decision, and I signed the paperwork, receiving a full scholarship.

## 6. 2X CHAMPION

I returned to Trinity Valley in good spirits, where my friends were waiting to hear the news. I happily told them I had signed with Tennessee, and they celebrated with joy. I finished my classes at Trinity Valley and graduated with zest.

The 2006-07 season was one of the most unforgettable seasons in my life. First, moving to Tennessee was a big step. It was the highlight of my career up to this point. I felt this opportunity was going to make me or break me. I had to learn my way around town again, just as I did when I was in Texas. After a short time, I got the hang of it and began my journey. I met new teammates and made new friends. I was officially a Lady Vol. Their basketball program started at the beginning of the twentieth century, in 1903, so they had a long history that I was proud to be a part of now. This would be my home for the next two years.

The Lady Vols casually gathered for the first time to feel each other out on the court before practice officially began. I was a bit nervous. A couple of players doubted my ability to help the team, but I was one to stand up for myself and not back down. I took the spotlight and did a little crossover and a swift handle that I knew they weren't used to seeing a female player execute. This gained me respect right away from the rest of the team.

To be honest, school was boring, and I didn't like class. I couldn't wait for practice to start. Playing basketball, I believe, is what motivated me to stay in school. I think if you find something you love to do and use that to motivate you to do well in school, you can make your dream come true. It's definitely hard work—they say that things worth having are never easy to get—but time moves more quickly than one would think.

Just take me, for example. Looking back on my childhood, my high school years, and even my time at junior college, I can't believe how fast everything passed. It felt like I had only blinked, and here I was. It was an amazing feeling to be on the team that I'd wanted to play with ever since I knew about basketball. I believed that things were just getting started, and I was ready to give it my all.

Summitt was no joke—at practice, I experienced a whole new side to her compared to what I'd seen a few months prior. She was serious. I was scared to laugh or smile; I didn't want to miss any drill or exercise. I was not going to let her to make an example out of me. There was so much pressure that I felt like I was in boot camp!

Luckily, I understood Coach Summitt. She held a reputation as one of the best college coaches in the world, and I was playing for her. I couldn't let her down. There was absolutely no room for error. We lifted weights, and they were heavy, but I had to get used to that. We had all types of strength and conditioning workouts that I had to adjust to, but I hung in there.

I found out that in twenty-nine years, Coach Summitt had never recruited a really short point guard or a junior college player—until I came along. I was an exception, and that made me realize just how lucky I was. She thought I was special, and I had to live up to her expectations. I was the shortest player on the team, but I made sure I played like one of the biggest.

As the season progressed, we built chemistry amongst ourselves and became dominant. We cut through teams like a hot knife through butter and played as if we'd been playing together for years. No one would have guessed that this was only our first year doing so. Imagine if I'd been there for the two years I had spent at Trinity Valley!

We had teams that gave us a good run such as LSU, Rutgers, Duke, North Carolina, and Stanford. In 2007, we lost to LSU in the SEC Tournament.

Every year during March, before the NCAA Tournament began, we had team gatherings at Coach Summitt's home for the Selection Show and the unveiling of the brackets with the sixty-four teams. There were four regional sites, and each team was seeded from one to sixteen, with one being the best team in that region.

We watched the show together as a team to see our placement and discover which teams we would play. We also watched for the matchups of other teams in our bracket in order to determine how to get to the Final Four. Once you lost a game in the NCAA tourney, you were done for the season. We usually ended up in a good spot, because we had a great overall record.

The early round games were the sub-regionals, followed by the regionals, and then the Final Four. Win six straight games, and your team was the National Champion. My junior year, we won every game fairly easily until we reached the Elite Eight. These eight teams were the best surviving teams from each bracket, and they then had to square off to get to the game's biggest stage: the Final Four.

We worked hard and believed we had the best team and coaching staff. It was our time to win. On the court, we reviewed how we would guard each player. Our preparation was on point. We made our way to the Final Four, and we were determined not to let it slip away. We played against North Carolina in the semifinal game and were down twelve points with eight minutes to go, but we held the Tar Heels to no field goals and just two free throws and won the game.

This led to the final game of that season—the 2007 National Championship matchups in Cleveland, Ohio against Rutgers. Winning a championship is a difficult task, but it is possible if you work hard, believe in yourself, and stay together as a team. That's just what we did. Our team worked together so well that it seemed as if it was meant to be.

We were on the same page, and we shared the same goal, which made it easier to work together to claim the 2007 national title.

One of the reasons I believe our team had such great chemistry was because we held each other accountable for our actions on and off the court. We challenged each other to deliver the best of our abilities. We even got together several times for team bonding. The team captains suggested the team come together once or twice a month to get to know each other better. During these gatherings we did things like watch movies, play cards, and just hang out. It was a great idea. We became tighter as a family, sharing sisterly bonds. Our respect, trust, and communication extended beyond the basketball court, making all of us play better together.

Everyone knew their roles and played to their strengths. We supported each other and helped one another whenever one of us struggled. If all of us struggled, well, we struggled together. I must give a lot of credit to the coaching staff as well. The coaches did a marvelous job of putting our particular team together to play for the national title. As one, we were unstoppable. We were destined to succeed.

The 2007 championship fell on a cold April day, and we were just about to enter the court to face Rutgers. The game would be televised on ESPN. I was ready for it. I had grown up with the girls from the Rutgers team and was familiar with them. As we entered the arena, which was full of Tennessee fans, I felt a chill come over me. The announcer called each of the starting players' names. I felt a jolt when I heard my name over the arena speakers. It was a once in a lifetime moment. I was nervous but confident, almost cocky. You couldn't really blame me; I felt like I had reached this point for a reason, and I had to win. This meant everything.

I greeted the roaring fans, feeling just as excited as they were. The arena in downtown Cleveland was huge—possibly the biggest stage I've ever played on in my career. It was packed, and the crowd was so loud we could hardly hear each other speak. We had to get close to each other to be heard or else try yelling over the screams of the fans. The seats were filled with the Lady Volunteer college colors of orange and white. I was astounded by how much support we had. All those fans gave me the utmost confidence, and my nervousness melted away until I felt like I was simply playing a home game in Tennessee.

The game started, and I knew someone had to set the tone, so I knocked down a three-pointer and applied tough defense to pressure my opponents. When we got the ball back, I set my teammate up for a two-pointer. We were on a roll now, and I was feeling good about it. I ran the floor the way Coach Summitt wanted me to and began raining three-pointers on Rutgers. We gained a lead, but Rutgers wasn't going to back off. The Scarlet Knights began catching up, and again I got us a cushion with a three-pointer. My teammates were doing a terrific job; Coach Summitt loved it, but kept her composure, knowing Rutgers was just as determined and focused as we were to win that game.

The second half began, and we were dominating the game. Every time Rutgers tried to come back, we scored again. As the game neared the end, I hit another three-pointer, and that closed the deal. It took a moment for it to sink in that we had won, with a final score of 59-46. The audience was screaming so loudly that I thought the arena walls would explode. There was so much emotion, I felt like I could burst. I ran and jumped into my teammates' arms, colorful confetti rained down on us, my ears rang with all the noise, and no one knew what to do or say—we were that happy.

The award stage was set for us, and we went to get our trophy. We were officially the 2007 NCAA National Champions. It was an incredible feeling— most certainly a proud one. The only thing going through my mind at that moment was: I did it. All my hard work paid off, and I won the championship. I did it!

I'd worked hard for this, and my determination helped me overcome all of the doubts and obstacles in my path. I hadn't allowed my anxiety, my insufficient SAT scores, or my height hold me back. I had helped the Lady Vols win the championship, the program's seventh national title, and the first one since 1998. Standing there on that stage as a winner with my team, I had proven that short people could succeed at basketball and make a difference, just the same as tall basketball players could. Coach Summitt was ecstatic that the Lady Vols had ended their championship drought, and I was just as delighted that she had believed enough in me to give me a chance at Tennessee. She had never once mentioned my height, and I am so grateful for her confidence.

I knew my hard work would pay off when my talent didn't always show up. After all, I once heard that "hard work beats talent when talent doesn't work hard." Ultimately, I have four championship rings to prove it—two from high school and two from the University of Tennessee. Not only did I earn these rings for being a champion, I even got the opportunity to visit the White House with my team.

We were honored at the White House after winning the 2007 National Championship. We took a plane to Washington, DC and dressed up in formal clothing for a meet-and-greet with President Bush. The White House, naturally, is like no other house

I've ever seen. For one thing, the building is huge; it is more like a mansion than a house.

When we arrived, I had already expected tight security, but I still managed to be surprised at just how much security actually surrounded the White House. The day was nice and warm—comfortable enough to have a picnic. A tour guide showed us around for a couple of hours, and then we took a photo with President Bush. It was one of the greatest and most memorable moments of my life and career.

In addition to meeting the president, I was chosen, along with teammate Nicky Anosike, to be put on the new practice facility wall called Pratt Pavilion on the Tennessee campus. The university needed a dedicated basketball practice facility, because the other campus gyms were often reserved for other sports. Coach Summitt also got her name on the court at Thompson-Boling Arena, where Tennessee plays its home games.

When I saw my picture on the wall in the Pratt Pavilion, I was shocked. All I could think was, "Wow, they chose me." The picture showed me going up for a right-hand layup, and I appreciated the gesture. I hadn't even been told that I would be put on the wall, and I'm still on that very same wall today. I am very thankful that I will always be remembered and seen at the University of Tennessee. That tells me that I did, indeed, have an impact there.

Another huge honor was being featured in the 2007
special spring issue of *Sports Illustrated* magazine.
The magazine ran a great story about the Lady Vols
with multiple photos, and it was extremely good
exposure for our team. The story detailed the Lady
Vols' winning the seventh national title after nine

long years. It made me feel successful. I was finally the winner I had always wanted to be. I always believed that great things come to those who work hard, and now I am a living testimony to that.

During the summer, I decided to stay in Tennessee and continue my schoolwork to prepare for my senior year. My academics still weren't the best, but I received tutoring and studied a lot on my own. I was progressing well, but I hadn't yet reached my main childhood goal—the WNBA.

Tension over what would happen after graduation was building for me. I wanted to be in the WNBA; that was something I had to achieve. Oftentimes I sat and thought about everything I had gone through as a child—namely, that feeling of being at your lowest point. It was a feeling I had experienced often when I was young, and it was something I never wanted to experience again. It was because of those times, though, that I was a stronger person mentally. I now had the power to cope with any struggle or situation.

Once I knew basketball could change my life, I wanted to make sure I showed the world the talent and skills that God blessed me with. I was determined to do well in life and live positively. Remembering how I used to constantly move from place to place and from school to school wasn't something I let drag me down. Instead, I used it for strength and as motivation to keep striving and reach my dreams.

As a child, it was hard for me to make new friends, adjust to change, and have a stable life. I wanted to be able to help my parents and make them happy, especially now that I was becoming successful. My parents had always inspired me to do well in life. This was my time to achieve great things, and I didn't want to let them down. I wanted to make them proud, and for once, allow them to live a happy life. I wanted to prove those other people wrong—the ones who thought I wouldn't be able to make it just because I was undersized. I felt like I could set a trend and make a difference in the sport, and in the world.

As I prepared for my senior year of college, I looked back on how each school year had developed me as a player and as a person. Having matured at a young age, I quickly learned how to prioritize responsibilities and how to work hard. I developed patience, I learned about different cultures, and now, I was finally in the stage of my life where I would learn independence.

Life is never perfect or easy, and everyone learns that at some point, but I believed I had everything I needed. I had the special gifts of confidence, belief, and faith (things people can lose too easily). I was fortunate enough to have the love of family and friends, all of whom wanted to see me do well in life. I was able to stay positive under pressure and negativity. It's those hard times that show your true character, and I was able to preserve my character during personal difficulties.

I was a year away from leaving college, and I wanted to show why I was different. I could see how strong I had been as a little girl growing up and how that had given me the strength I have today. Basketball challenged me as a point guard. I had to be able to multitask by balancing schoolwork with basketball. At each turning point in my life, all of the obstacles I faced were worth the battle because it brought out the best in me. I now know what hard work is all about, and I wouldn't have made it if I hadn't had God or my supporting cast: my parents.

Fall came around, and classes began. It felt good to know this was my final year. The days were long, tiring, and repetitive: classes all day, hours of basketball practice afterwards. Finding time to study was difficult, but it was a priority; I didn't want any failing grades. I couldn't afford anything to jeopardize my chance to graduate.

The most exhausting days were game days that fell on school days—both at home and on road trips— after the 2007-08 basketball season began. I am not a big traveler, so if it had been up to me, I would only play all home games. But instead, I obviously had to play some games at home and others at opponents' arenas. Even though we traveled on a chartered plane and didn't have to wait in line to go through security, I still dreaded the travel days. During road trips we had a full schedule planned: mandatory breakfast, lunch, practice, dinner, and study hall. We had curfew, and our phones had to be turned in by a certain time at night. I did not have much leisure time, because I was so tired and needed to sleep, and the next day would be game day.

There were a couple of new members added to our team, but we were still the same power-packed Lady Vols. We played out the season competitively, facing LSU a second time for the SEC tournament championship. For us, it was payback time. There was no way we would let this team beat us for the SEC tournament title two years in a row. This time, we came to win.

Our next step was the National Championship. The 2008 Final Four was held in Tampa, Florida that year. I had never been to the Sunshine State, and all

I could think of was beautiful weather, great beaches, and lots of people, stuff to do, and a beautiful hotel. I was determined to stay focused, because I knew the Lady Vols and I were there on an unfinished business trip; we wanted to repeat as champions.

I didn't come this far to lose. I stayed focused and didn't leave the hotel unless it was for a team function. All the Lady Vol fans were very supportive and followed us everywhere we played. We felt like every game was a home game and saw so much orange and white in Tampa. Florida is a beautiful state, and being there with all the sunshine kept me in high spirits. We played LSU in the Final Four and won on a last-second shot, making it to the National Championship game. We were going against Stanford, an exceptional team that had beaten us earlier that season.

The day before the big game, both teams had a lot of media and team stuff to handle before we had time for ourselves. I followed my own day-before-game-day ritual that I liked to do. I relaxed in my hotel or home, depending on where the game was, and listened to music. I enjoyed texting and talking on the phone with family and friends. I did not like to be distracted or waste a lot of energy before a game. I have always been pretty simple: I like to eat a good meal and get plenty of rest the night before a game so that I have a lot of energy.

We were all looking forward to the game. We headed into the packed arena and were immediately met with cheers from the crowd. Tipoff was scheduled for 7:00 p.m., and the game was nationally televised. Everyone was eager to see if the Lady Volunteers could do it again. Our names were called, and we came out onto the court. Once the whistle blew, it was game on.

I was determined to take home this championship for Tennessee. There is nothing like winning a championship, especially in your senior year; that feeling of accomplishment in finally fulfilling your goals is pure bliss. This game in particular tested my abilities. For me, it was the game I grew the most from in college.

I was determined not to have any slip-ups like I did when Tennessee faced the Arizona State women's basketball team, which was my first road game as a Lady Vol in the 2006-07 season. Playing against the Sun Devils had been a challenge for me. Their team was athletic, well coached, and tenacious on defense. I've never been played quite that way before, so it was a surprise. I was used to playing at my home arena and hearing our team song, "Rocky Top." When I faced Arizona State, a team even tougher than I was, and was not able to hear that song, it actually came as a total shock.

The crowd had been extremely aggressive at that game, but luckily, we still had a lot of orange in the stands. The Sun Devils were very physical, but we ended up winning the game, 83-74; however, I knew I had played my worst game ever. With it having been such a big game—on the road and televised—I didn't know if I was built for this type of environment or for elite Division I women's basketball. Very passive, I was not the normal Shannon Bobbitt that game. I had a few turnovers, and my defense was not good enough to frustrate the other point guard and disrupt her ball handling. I had not made any shots. Mentally, I had just not been into the game. This game was a wake-up call for me, and after it was over, I immediately asked Coach Summitt if I could watch the film of it so I could correct mistakes and be prepared for other tough road games. I knew from that game forward that I could not play badly or be unfocused if I wanted to lead my team.

After the game, I met with my coach, and we watched the movie together. Coach Summitt explained to me that if I was going to be her starting point guard, I couldn't play at such a low level. And she was right. I was better than what I had showed at that game, and I assured her it wouldn't happen again. In Pat Summitt's book, *Sum it Up* (2013), the head coach said that I exhausted myself on the practice court to pay her back for taking a chance on me. She called me a sponge for instruction who did exactly what she asked. "I'd adopt you if I could," Summitt told me.

I immediately got back in the gym and worked on my game, preparing my mind for the kind of physicality and intense pressure that I knew would come now. From that day forward, I became a tough point guard. I learned to be ready for war every time I stepped out on the court.

I became well aware that there were other players just like me who wanted to prove they were better. But I was now built for these situations both on and off the court. I was ready for Stanford, and I gave them my best. I made sure I shot my three-pointers with confidence; my defense was outstanding, my offense was terrific, and my passes were on target. I even took it to the basket on them. The Cardinals couldn't stop me. My goal was to shut down their point guard and make her fumble the ball. Her shots weren't falling, so I knew I had to keep pressure on her.

We beat Stanford and won the game, 64-48, becoming the 2008 national champions. Pat Summitt had challenged us to hold Stanford under 50 points, and we did. Winning a second consecutive championship felt like another dream come true. I had helped to lead the University of Tennessee to another title, and I am sure a lot of people had thought I could not do it. God has blessed me in such a special way that it is unbelievable.

The arena was filled with orange and white. The diehard fans made the game a lot easier, because we saw that we had people supporting us and believing we could win. I was happy I had been able to come to the program and make a difference, and even more excited to end my college career on a winning note—both on and off the court. That day will be one to remember for the rest of my life. Our banners will hang in the rafters at school, and we will always will be honored and remembered as winners.

Once again President Bush at the White House honored us, but this time, I wasn't able to attend because I was getting ready for the WNBA. I felt like my chances of making it were very good, but I didn't want to watch the draft because, although I was confident, I wasn't sure if I'd be chosen. So instead I asked my parents to keep me informed about draft developments. They faithfully sat in front of the television, anxious to hear my name.

The picks were being announced, but there still was no "Shannon" called. The first round ended. I had wanted to be called in the first round, but I would take what came and proceed from there. That was what I learned in junior college: you have to start somewhere and make it work; start your climb from anywhere.

The second round began. My parents became restless as they watched, worrying that my dream would not come true. They wondered how to break the bad news to me if this happened. What would I do then? But good fortune was upon me. In the second round, they heard that the Los Angeles Sparks had selected Shannon Bobbitt.

Cries of joy were heard down the hallway of my building in New York, and even people outside were buzzing about the big announcement. My parents called me as soon as they heard my name in the draft, but I was on a flight back to Tennessee from Tampa and couldn't receive any calls. Once I landed, my phone was going crazy; everyone wanted to be the first to give me the news that would solidify my dream. I had officially become part of the WNBA.

I can't explain how much joy I felt when I heard I had been drafted. I could have fallen right there; I was floating on clouds. My prayers had been answered. I had made it. My confidence had helped me through my career in college. Though I was still tired from the games and the effort, I was over the moon. All my hard work on the court had finally paid off for me.

After playing for one of the toughest coaches in the world, and after all the struggles I had faced in childhood, I knew there wasn't anything in life I couldn't achieve. I was nervous, but ready. I was looking forward to preparing for the WNBA. My own dream turned out to be real—to be true. I dreamed that I'd play in the WNBA someday, and now I would do so.

One of my favorite quotes states, "Tough times don't last, but tough people do." If you set your goal and never give up, no matter what anyone tells you, you'll make it. Having determination, a strong work ethic, and confidence are all very important, but believing in yourself is the key. So if you have a dream, find the truth and pursue it, and make that truth a reality.

# 7. THE VALUE OF NOTHING

After hearing my name in the draft and knowing where I would play during the summer, I still had to graduate from the University of Tennessee that spring of 2008. I only had a few weeks to regroup from a long, successful college career before I entered the real business world. I was extremely excited and nervous at the same time; I didn't know what to expect. I was staying ready for whatever was going to be thrown my way, whether it was good or bad. I got a call from the head coach of the LA Sparks, Michael Cooper. I was excited to be talking with a champion himself and hearing all the things he was saying to me as he welcomed me over the phone to the training camp, telling me to just relax and have fun—and be myself.

I was also excited to be playing alongside great players like Lisa Leslie, Delisha Milton-Jones, Marie Ferdinand-Harris, and my college teammate Candace Parker. I flew home from college and received many text messages, emails, and calls from family and friends about taking my talents into the WNBA. I did as much as I could while I was home, spending time with loved ones and hanging out with friends in New York City. I was eating my favorite meals, packing, getting my hair done, and of course still working out. I knew I was going to spend the rest of my summer in Los Angeles, California. The season lasts about four or five months, and though it usually seemed really short, but this time it felt so long.

When the day came for me to head to California, I told my family and friends farewell, and I was on my way. My flight to California was the longest I had ever been on, lasting for about six hours—and Lord knows I hate long flights. The turbulence is what scares me the most. I would rather drive twenty hours than fly for a few, but the flight was a smooth ride, and actually relaxing.

I finally landed in California, and when I got to LA, I could immediately tell it was different. I was used to walking everywhere, but not in California—you definitely needed a car.

Once I arrived at LAX, I had someone there to pick me up and take me to my hotel to meet the manager and coaches. I also got a physical to make sure I was cleared to practice. I had a few days before the first official practice started, but I wasn't yet guaranteed a spot on the team. The training camp lasted for about three weeks, and we had two practices per day for three hours each. I was so tired by the time we finished on the fourth day of practice. I was competing for a spot on the roster, though, so I couldn't complain about anything. Taking days off meant getting cut, and that meant food would be taken off of my table and from my family.

By the end of the first week, and as we entered the second week of practice, players were getting cut left and right; the circle was becoming smaller and smaller every day. I tried not to build friendships and get comfy with the players at training camp, because when they got cut, it became an emotional day for people. I had to remember it was a business, and when there is money involved, everything is fair game and survival of the fittest. The WNBA is not as big as the NBA, so there were limited spots on the roster. The Sparks had to trim theirs down from sixteen to thirteen players and send it into the main office. Wondering every day whether you are going to get cut and be sent home can wreck your brain. There was a lot of tension and pressure every single day. The coaches and managers were always watching and talking, determining who would make the team. Some players get really scared and messed up a lot, even though they really were good players. When the pressure is on and people are watching you, the first thing that comes to mind is, "Are they talking about me?" which then leads to questions like, "Will I make the team? Will they call me into office to cut me? I hope I am playing well." The thoughts go on and on.

There are many different reasons why players get cut. It can be money situations, positions, injury, or you can just get outworked in practice. During the whole training camp, I stayed in the hotel, because I had to prove myself. Once I made the team, I was taken to my apartment and given a car. It was a nice one-bedroom apartment, fully furnished. That was the first time I experienced really living alone.

Every team roster was set and ready for the season. We had an unbelievable team on paper and were even picked to win the 2008 championship.

My first year was a learning experience for me. I had great point guards in front of me, but I continued to compete and earn my respect and playing time. Playing professional basketball was a lot different than I thought, especially comparing it to college. The money was the main difference. Also, in the WNBA, not everyone was entitled to have the same things, like in college (as far as apparel). The top players on the team had sneaker endorsements and gear. On the court, women were a lot bigger and stronger, and their minds were sharp because of their experience playing professionally. They knew how to win games and how things worked at a higher level. So, that was an adjustment for me throughout the season. Although the season moved along quickly, it seemed slow at times. I had to get better every single day and learn the players and plays quickly, or I would be left behind.

The season was short, so I had to learn, remember what I had learned, and move forward. I had to watch a lot of films, because there weren't a lot of teams in the league, so every team was scouting each player's weaknesses and strengths. I also had to learn the team plays and concepts. Your IQ had to be high in this game, because you had to outthink the opponent since they already knew the play calls you were ready to execute. I watched films on all the players I would have to face, studying their strengths and weaknesses. The season started, and players were performing well individually—but as a team, it wasn't so great. We lacked the chemistry that we had been trying to build throughout the whole training camp. During that time, it had been challenging to build chemistry, because there were always changes being made to the roster. On top of that, any day throughout the season, a player could be traded or cut. I faced a lot of ups and downs, and losses and wins, but that's what built my character; it was the adversity. Some games I would play more minutes than other games, and some games I wouldn't play at all during my rookie season. It was also the first time I experienced playing back-to-back games. Being a professional athlete proved to be very difficult after a while. We could have a game Monday night at home in LA, and then have a game Tuesday night all the way on the east coast against the New York Liberty, so flying and preparing for the next opponent became very tiring and took a toll on our bodies. As professionals, we had to learn how to take care of our bodies – eating well, drinking enough water, taking the proper treatments, and getting the proper rest. In the WNBA, if you didn't take care of your body, you could lose to a team due to tiredness and fatigue alone. Very few players were able to withstand that pressure and strain on the mind, body, and soul.

My team held up and took pretty good care of their bodies, and it helped that I was on a team with mostly veterans. Every season there is a WNBA All Star break, and players who are not selected in the All Star game have a few days off to spend at home with family. That year, the All Star break took place around the midpoint of the season. All the All-Star players who were selected had a great first half of the season.

The second part of the season started, and I became the starting point guard for the rest of the season. I had to run the team the best way I knew how and please all four of the superstars on my team. I never thought it would be so difficult pleasing my teammates, because I was the type of point guard to whom this came naturally, but when you have four players who want the ball—or feel they should always have the ball—well, there was only one basketball, so it became a problem for me, especially as a rookie. I just wanted to play the game the right way and find a way to win. I looked for the mismatch and who had the hot hand that game, and I had to learn quickly how to keep all of my teammates happy. I finished out the season as the starting point guard knowing I had led my team as far as I could, but we fell short from winning the championship.

We lost in the western conference finals, which is a best out of three series. (The WNBA finals are best out of five.) During the season we played against one of the best teams in the league that year, the Detroit Shock. Their nickname was The Bad Girls, because they played dirty and were very aggressive players offensively and defensively. It was a tough battle, seeing two great NBA legends go at it on the sidelines coaching their teams and the great players on the court competing and battling for the win. These were the most physical games I played the whole season. I was the smallest player on the court, and I was a rookie, so I was not going to get any calls. I would attack the basket and get hit, and the referee would not call anything. I would look at the referee as if to say, "Are you going to call something? I am getting fouled." One referee, whom I will never forget, said, "Rookie, step your weight up." I was so shocked, and I looked at her like, you come out here and play against me—you would have to step your weight up. From that day forward, I grew up fast. It was a woman's game, and I was fine with it, because I was well prepared and ready for all the physicality I was facing. I just wasn't sure if the other players were ready for my kind of street ball play.

The referees didn't control the game from the beginning. The game got so physical and personal it led to a team brawl. Players started going after each other to fight. I was on the bench when the fight broke out between my teammate and a player from the Shock. I ran off the bench and hit their assistant coach. It wasn't the smartest thing to do; it was just my reaction. It was my instinct—I just ran over and hit him. After the altercation I was suspended for two games and fined a lot of money, and one of the games I was suspended for was my debut home game that was to be held in front of my family and friends. I was so sad I couldn't play. I wanted to play in my hometown at Madison Square Garden, even though I knew there would be another opportunity for me to play in front of my family and friends.

The season was over. I thought it had been a good season, and a wake-up call for me. I was solid the whole season, and I worked hard. I had seen what I needed to work on and knew what to expect for the next season. After every season there is an exit meeting to discuss your performance with the coaches and manager so that they can evaluate you for that season. I had my exit meeting, and it went well; I spoke about the things I needed to work on and what I thought about the season. I packed my bags and got ready for my flight back to NYC to prepare for my first season overseas: I had signed with my first team in Turkey. I was looking forward to the experience, but wasn't looking forward to the distance from my family, or the long flight.

Most WNBA players play overseas after the season is over. The WNBA season goes from May to September, and then the players head overseas from October to April, depending on how many months was agreed in the contract. Some countries only have a four-month season, like Korea and China.

I dreaded my flights overseas, but it was a part of my job and a way to make money and take care of my family, so I had to do what I had to do. I got on my flight to Istanbul, Turkey, which lasted about twelve hours. When I got there, no one spoke English well, so it was difficult to get help. I said a prayer and stayed as calm as I could. The manager from the club was there to pick me up and take me to meet the coach and my teammates. I immediately had to undergo a physical exam and start practice the next day. They sure didn't waste any time! Thankfully, the manager knew some English, so whenever there was an issue, I was able to speak with him. A few of my teammates knew a little English, and they were able to explain what the coaches said.

In my free time, I listened to music, read books, and wrote as I normally do in my journal. The time difference between Turkey and NYC was seven hours, and I was so tired when practice started because of the jetlag. It took me about a month to adjust to the time in Turkey. It took me a while to adjust to the food, as well. I wasn't used to the smell of the food, and I didn't enjoy the taste. Consequently, I filled up on fruits, veggies, and lots of juices and water until one of my teammates helped me find a restaurant that served chicken and rice with veggies and bread. I fell in love with the restaurant and ate there almost every day until I became familiar with other places nearby.

Things were getting better. I was learning some of the language and the Turkish culture. I watched lots of movies and TV shows on my computer and called my family on Skype whenever they were up. Seeing them and speaking with them kept me sane.

Practices were easy. I didn't expect it to be so physical, but it was. The style of play was very aggressive: players were able to hand check you, bump you, push you, and referees would not make a call. Luckily I was used to that kind of play, because I am a physical player. We had a good, solid team and competed every day in practices and in games. Although we made the playoffs, we fell short in the first round.

The money was good, and the people in the city loved the women's basketball team. They were very supportive. When I stepped on the court I showed love back as well, because I am a crowd pleaser, an entertainer, and a winner. The fans were very interesting. They shouted at the other team's players and fans, throwing things on the court, screaming, arguing—it was just a lot of crazy stuff I wasn't used to seeing, but I loved it. They were into the game for sure.

We didn't get cars because it was very dangerous to drive in that city. Everything was within walking distance, and if we needed something that wasn't, the manager would go and get it for us. We had two practices a day, and we played once a week. The weather was nice; it did get cold, but it was weather I could handle. When there was a storm, it rained for a long time, and hard, too. The language was difficult to learn. I wanted to learn just the basic

words like "yes," "no," "hi," "bye," "thank you,"
and "Where is my money?" Those were the most
important to me while I was there. It was a business
trip, not a vacation, for me.

We traveled by planes and busses, depending on the
distance of our opponents. I didn't play against other
countries; I just competed throughout Turkey.
When the team was late paying my salary, I
immediately contacted my agent, who handled the
situation. My agent told me not to practice or play
in games until I received payment, and if I had had
to sit out long enough, I probably would have
traveled back home and sued the team. Thankfully
it never got that far, but I did sit out a few times due
to such a money situation.

It was a good experience for my first time overseas;
I enjoyed my coach and teammates. As Christmas
break approached I dreaded the long flight home,
but I knew I needed to go. I wanted to see my
family, get my hair done, eat, and rest. When I got
home, I didn't even want to come back to Turkey,

but I had to, or my contract would have been terminated, which meant I wouldn't get paid. I was able to go home for just a week.

One thing I realized at that time was that I didn't know how to cook. The chances I'd had to learn from my parents, I hadn't taken advantage of. Instead, I had just wanted to go play basketball. Anytime I was overseas, I had to spend money to eat or rely on my teammates to cook a good meal for dinner. I was either too tired or just too lazy to try to cook. I wanted to stay focused.

The season finally ended. I had played well and enjoyed the experience, but it was time to head back to the states for the summer.

# 8. ONE OPPORTUNITY ONE LIFETIME

Now my second year was starting up with the Sparks in the 2009 season, and that meant long, hard work for training camp. I was a little more familiar with the system, coaches, and the returning players this time around. I knew I had to prepare for being the starting point guard and getting my team to the championship game so we could have another chance to win. The team was not the same; a few players had been traded and cut, and new players were signed to the team. The coaches felt that this team was a stronger one and that we would have a better chance to win a championship. There were two practices a day, which were three hours long each. I competed once again for the starting position and playing time on the court. I made the team again, and our first game was on national television. I was excited and told everyone I knew.

So, extra pressure was put on me. I didn't win the starting point guard job. When game time came, I didn't get in the game at all; everyone else played but me, but I didn't know why. I was shocked by the decisions that were made, because I worked extremely hard and was getting better every day. I immediately went home and called my parents to vent. They were always there for me when I needed to shed my tears, talk about my feelings, and let my anger out. From that moment on, I was prepared for anything and everything to happen to me—even the things that I did not agree with. I lived on the edge my whole season with the Sparks, never knowing what to expect—except, that is, the mind games within the business. Most of the decisions that were made against me were out of my control, and that made me more upset and angry, because I couldn't change the outcome or situation.

We added an Olympian, Tina Thompson, to the team that season. Once again, we looked great on paper, and once again, we were picked to win the championship. Lisa Leslie also announced she would retire that season, and that gave us more motivation to play hard and win for her on her way out of the league.

My teammate, Ferdinand-Harris, was a great mentor to me at that time; she was a great player and an even better person. She wanted to see me do well on and off the court—in life, period. She shared some great knowledge with me, including some of her experiences playing in the league, and how she was able to play for several years and stay healthy. She gave me great advice, and we shared great laughs together. She definitely gave me hope and inspiration to do well that season.

I kept the same routine I'd had the previous season with the Sparks, traveling here and there, playing tough games every night—some won, some lost. I practiced hard every day, watched films, and went home to relax, though I always stayed on my toes—any day I could be cut, for whatever reason. I didn't have much time for pleasure, because I felt like if I had too much fun, it could cost me my career, and I would probably never bounce back. I never knew how to balance having fun or my personal life with my business life, because I was always busy and focused on being the best player I could be in the game of basketball. Even so, the weather in California was very nice almost every day, and I went to the beach several times, both during the day and at night. It was probably the highlight of my time living there. I didn't get out much other than that, because I didn't make friends outside of my teammates, and I was more of a homebody.

The beach was unbelievable. I loved the view; it was very calm and relaxing for my mind. When I was bored, I took long rides along the beach or relaxed at home and listened to music. California was very different from NYC. To my relief, I never witnessed an earthquake during my stay there, as I can recall. One of my favorite fast food places was called "IN & OUT." It was a great burger spot.

My parents came out to visit me in California, as did my siblings. I was so excited and happy to see them, and finally got a few home-cooked meals.

Coach Summitt also came out to watch the Sparks play, and it was great to see her. Playing in the Staples Center arena was a great feeling. The lights were very bright, and celebrities came out to our games. I met so many celebrities, and when we met, we acted as if we had known each other for years. I met Snoop Dogg, Deebo (from the movie *Friday*), Tank, Kobe, Magic Johnson, and Halle Berry, just to name a few.

One day we had a game, and Halle Berry came out to see us play. I was so nervous because I knew she was watching us play, and I didn't even play that much in the game; I was so upset. The little time I did get when I was on the court I made sure I was noticed. I played with so much energy—I was just like a little kid out there again, having fun. When the game was over, we all went into the locker room, and Halle Berry came in. I was just sitting there thinking about the game and why I didn't play, and Halle Berry said, "Shannon, did you hear me screaming and cheering for you? You did well!" My reply was something like, "Really? Aww, thank you so much," and I asked her for a hug—and she gave me one. I was happy.

My team was a veteran team; we had great players and a great coaching staff, but for some reason we could not put the puzzle together and win a championship. That season I was able to play in my hometown at Madison Square Garden in front of family and friends, but I didn't perform well; I guess I was a little too anxious. They say pressure bursts pipes and makes diamonds, and for that game pressure really did burst the pipes, because I was not making shots and was not playing Bobbitt's game.

We made it to the western conference finals once more—the second year in a row—but fell short again. In the WNBA, teams are always scouting the players they are about to play against so that their defensive schemes are on point. As a result they knew all of our plays, so in preparing for each game we had to adjust to our plays and find better ways to score the ball. All of the teams were good; there wasn't one team that was better than the others. Everyone brought their "A" game when they knew they were playing against the Sparks, and the stands were always packed.

As a point guard in the league, I always had a tough opponent to battle. My confidence was up and down because of my playing time and the things that had happened to me thus far in the league. I wasn't playing Bobbitt's basketball; I was playing more like a robot. There wasn't one specific point guard that was tougher for me to play than the rest, but I am sure I was the opponent's worst nightmare when I stepped out onto the court.

Every team in the WNBA was known for different things they did well. For example, the Silver Stars was a great team that played well together. They shared the ball and always took care of the ball, and they hardly ever made mistakes. We had to be ready for great defense, and we especially had to communicate well when playing against them.

On the other hand, when playing against the
Phoenix Mercury you had to be ready to run a track
race and guard the three-point line because they
were a running team. So, every game was a tough
battle. One of the hardest arenas to play in was the
Key Arena, which was home to the Seattle Storm—
a great team. They had some loyal fans that
believed in them every game. Their fans were loud
and obnoxious, but very supportive. It was hard to
beat them on their home court.

The hardest part for me in the league was the mental
aspect. The skills, talents, speed, and strength
weren't issues for me; I was fit for all of those
areas. As long as I stayed healthy and gained more
experience on the court while playing, I felt I was
going to get better every year and eventually be one
of the top point guards in the league. I am a team
player who loves to learn. I was not used to losing;
my whole life I had been a winner while playing
basketball. But at the pro level, sometimes even
losing is considered winning, because you learn so
much, and you work extra hard on the weaknesses

you have as a team and individually. I had to grow up fast in the league. I had to learn not to take things so personally. Both Coach Summitt as well as my parents had prepared me for the next level as far as the foundation of working hard and putting my priorities first was concerned. My parents had taught me all about discipline and facing adversity, while Summitt had prepared me for handling pressure on the court, leading the team, being vocal, and understanding the game better.

In the league, a typical day included practice in the morning for two to three hours, and then after practice I had to shower, eat, and get physical treatment if needed. In addition to that, I often had an appearance I had to attend. If you missed those you would get fined, so you had to be on time. Afterwards, I typically had a few hours to do personal things like rest, watch films, or worked more on my craft if that was the day's schedule. There was time for another meal right before the evening practice, so I could have the energy to practice hard. After the evening practice was over, I showered, ate, and got physical treatment, and by the time I looked at the clock it would be 10:00 or 11:00 p.m.: time to go to sleep and get ready for the next morning's practice.

The league has lots of rules to follow, as does each individual team. At the time, I often felt like a little kid with all the rules I had to follow (not following the rules meant paying a fine). One day we had an away game and fell short in that game. My teammate and I went to sleep really late, and come morning I already had my things packed, but my teammate didn't. I warned her to have her things packed and ready for in the morning, because we had an early flight. The flight was at about 8:00 a.m., but we had to get on the bus at about 6:00 a.m. to make it to the airport in time. That morning, neither one of us heard the alarm go off; all we heard was the phone ringing, and one of our teammates said, "What are you guys doing? We are downstairs on the bus, waiting," and we jumped up and started getting dressed so fast! I was so nervous; my body was shaking because I knew we were going to get fined and miss the bus, and probably the flight. I immediately started brushing my teeth and getting dressed at the same time, falling down and everything, while my teammate was over there packing, trying to close her suitcase. I was yelling at her and saying, "Come on!" She was a rookie, so if we were late, it would have been my fault. I told her, "Forget that, get dressed! I will go downstairs and stall for a little more, and say you are coming down." I didn't want the team or the coaches to know we had just woken up, but we still had two minutes before the bus was going to take off. My rookie came running and breathing hard on the bus, and I said, "Rook, be quiet, control your breathing." Everyone was looking at us, and I was laughing. I was happy we didn't get fined, because it was after a loss, so the coach was in a bad mood. That was one of the funniest moments I'd experienced on the road. My teammates and I laughed about it all the time.

The season was finally over, and once again we had individual exit meetings with the coaches and the general manager. This time, my talk with the general manager was not so good. Her exact words to me were, "Bobbitt, if you don't come back as a better player, I will cut you." I will never forget those words. I responded respectfully, but in my mind, I felt I had been growing as a player. I came home after that tough season to regroup, spend time with my family, and get ready to head overseas again. I had a week or two to relax and train before I left.

That season I signed a contract to play in Israel. Before I headed to Israel, I had to ask a few people about the team, the city it was in, and the country itself. I heard it was a smaller version of NYC. It was described as a small city; every team was near each other. The country was extremely Americanized. The food was good and many people spoke English.

My flight was twelve hours long, with no layover; I was happy about that. It was a smooth ride, but too long. I stayed in a five-star hotel; it was very nice, and I loved everything about it. I had fun with the Americans on my team. They were very friendly, and good players, as well. The weather was really mild, and I was able to drive in this country. I shared the car with another American on my team. The routine I had in Israel was pretty much the same as the routine I had in Turkey. We played once a week, and practiced the rest of the days.

I loosened up a little and went out more in Israel than I did in Turkey. My favorite spot to eat was called Dixie. They served breakfast all day long. It was great to hang out and have fun with other Americans. I can say this country was the best by far for having fun, compared to the other countries in which I played. However, I didn't get a chance to visit a lot of the historical sites in Israel, such as Jerusalem and the Dead Sea. The next opportunity I get, I will make that a priority on my list. There wasn't a high level of competition there, but we still had good games. The Israelis were very aggressive, as well—they played a very physical game. The language was hard to learn, so I just learned the basic words and phrases to get me by while I was playing. There were a lot of familiar faces playing in Israel. Because I knew many people, I felt comfortable most of time. It made my stay enjoyable.

We started the season off well, winning our first three games in a row. I was happy. Then we lost the next three games. The coach immediately felt he had to make a change, and the decision he made was to cut me from the team. I was embarrassed, shocked, and upset, and the first thing I did was call my family. They talked me through it, as they normally did, and one thing they told me was that people do make mistakes, every day in life, and in the game of basketball there was no difference. I understood my parents.

I had now experienced being cut from an overseas team. I stayed in Israel for a few days, and my agent found me another job, which was in Poland—now one of my least favorite countries to play in. The Polish language was very difficult to learn, the games were highly competitive, and the weather was freezing; it felt worse than NYC. Aside from myself, there were two other Americans on my team.

This time, I had my own apartment and my own car. The only problem was that the car was a manual, and I had never learned how to drive a stick. My coach tried teaching me for a few minutes, but that wasn't nearly enough practice or training; I needed more time. My teammate tried to teach me, but it was just too difficult. One day I decided to take the car to practice. Practice started at 6:00 p.m., and I left at 4:00 p.m., just to make sure I made it on time. The gym wasn't that far away—maybe a ten-minute drive. Things didn't go well. The car kept stalling on me in middle of the street, the cars behind me were blowing their horns, and I was nervous, mad, and laughing, all at the same time. That was the first and last time I drove that car. I left it parked in front of my apartment, and I walked to practice every day.

I found a good restaurant near my apartment where I ate salmon and other fish almost every day. I was lonely and bored in Poland, but at the same time I was stressed. One night I decided to eat a bowl of cereal because I was hungry and it was too late to go out. My parents had sent it to me in a nice care package. Several minutes after I started eating it, I began to feel sick; the milk was spoiled.

I went to the restroom and started throwing up, and I hadn't done my hair in weeks so, at the same time, my hair was all tangled and coming out. I got on Skype with my parents, crying. They felt so bad for me, but they couldn't do anything to help me. When I got sick, I called my coaches and told them. They came to get me and take me to the hospital. I was given an IV, and afterwards I felt much better. The milk didn't have a bad smell, but next time I will pay more attention to the expiration date.

I had a good season in Poland, but I was happy to see it come to an end; I was ready to leave. The WNBA draft was going on back at home. I wasn't able to watch who the Sparks were going to draft, but I was anxious and patiently waiting to read it online. The draft finished, and the Sparks had drafted a point guard. I knew I was in for war and had to come prove myself, but my season abroad ended later than I had expected, and training camp was going to be over in a couple of days. I had received many emails and text messages about the Sparks drafting a point guard. I knew my job was on the line.

# 9. BASKETBALL LOVE AFFAIR

Remembering what my meeting was like at the end of my second year with the Sparks, I wanted to prove I was a better player. I only had a few days to do so, though, because I came late into training camp due to the delayed finish with my season overseas in Poland. I competed, but it didn't seem as if I was pleasing the coaches or even grabbing their attention. It was just a gut feeling I had. The last day of training camp arrived, and the final roster had to be submitted to the main office from all the teams in the league. We finished the last practice, but I wasn't called to the office. Even so, I still had a bad feeling; something was telling me they were going to call me.

When I got home I just sat there, thinking to myself about my performance during the last few days of practice. I hadn't been myself; I was too worried about being cut. I wasn't playing Bobbitt basketball. My phone rang. I answered, and the general manager said, "Bobbitt, I am coming to you. I want to speak to you." I said, "Okay, cool." I came downstairs, and we began to talk. She said she had made other plans; she had to cut me, because she was getting a player from another team. I thanked her, but the whole time I was trying not to cry. I was told that a few of my teammates had recommended the player from the other team. It was hard, but I knew it was a business after all, and all I could do was pack my things and be out of the apartment the next day because the new players were ready to move in. I called my parents and once again cried and vented about my emotions. I spoke to close friends and family about what had happened, and they were there to support me and share their opinions and advice with me. Talking with all of them helped me a lot; I was just so upset, and I really didn't think I would be cut after coming so far. I was completely losing my confidence; I wanted to give up and not play any longer. I was mentally hard on myself and took things personally, even though I knew it wasn't personal.

I flew home to spend the summer with my family and continue to train. I couldn't just sit back and wait for a call about another opportunity in the league. There wasn't another WNBA team interested in me, so I decided to sit out the entire 2010 season. I didn't even want to go outside, because I was always getting questions. Why are you not in the league? Why are you home? What happened? I just didn't want to talk about anything. While I was home, I used that time to reflect on how my career was going, what was going wrong, and what I needed to change. I thought about the youth, my family, observing everything, and saying to myself that I wouldn't wish this feeling or situation on anyone, because I felt like my basketball career was over before it really got started. I wanted to share my story; I felt like it would make me feel better and touch the hearts and lives of the youth. I decided to start my own basketball foundation by doing clinics and camps for the underprivileged kids who were not on any organized teams and felt that they didn't have anything to do outside. I started the Shannon Bobbitt Foundation for young ballers' basketball clinics and camps, open to boys and girls ages seven through eighteen. This made me feel good, for sure.

Giving back always made me happy. I always loved putting smiles on people's faces and making a difference in the world. I showed the kids both basketball and life skills. I spoke to them about what it took to become a pro and what it took to stay a pro. I shared my experience about being cut, how I felt, and my daily workouts. I told them school was the key. Knowledge is power, along with hard work and confidence. All the kids had dreams in life they could fulfill, but they had to believe they could achieve those dreams—especially when times got hard.

That year, I held two basketball clinics in my neighborhood. I bought shirts, medals, certificates, beverages, and other things for the events. The clinics were held outside, and we had a great turnout—about seventy-five kids total. We took pictures, I signed autographs, and most importantly, they had fun and learned a lot about what it took to become a pro on and off the court. I enjoyed myself, and giving back actually made me feel a lot better. Not having as much time to think about having been cut or dwelling on why I wasn't in the league helped as well.

I watched the WNBA games to stay in the loop, see what each team was doing, and figure out where I could see myself playing. I was best at doing my own homework and was determined to get back into the league. I continued to work out twice a day, at 6:00 a.m. and 6:00 p.m. I didn't give up; I continued to strive. Adversity sure builds character, because I was becoming mentally strong day by day. The summer was over, and it was time to head overseas again. I was finally able to be playing once more.

Same country, same goals, but a different team—everything was the same routine when I went to Israel again. I was familiar with the culture, the people, and the city, but I had to get used to the new coach and the new team. We had a solid team, but not good enough to win a championship. We won many games, but we also lost many games we shouldn't have lost. One thing about Israel is that the coaches are quick to cut players after one or two losses. We lost a couple of games, and again, I was cut. I really couldn't figure out why I was always the one getting cut. I know I can't win games alone.

I felt embarrassed and wondered whether this would be the story of my basketball career. I started to question myself more and more and completely doubted myself; there was a lot going on in my mind. I knew I had great skills and talents. My attitude was good; I was always a professional. I was also fortunate to have great people in my corner who always reassured me, believed in me, and encouraged me not to quit, because there were plenty of times I wanted to give up and just throw in the towel.

There were people who told me the truth about myself as a player and what I needed to improve, and even though it wasn't about my character as a player and the information was hard to hear, I still respected the advice and felt better at end of the day. My job should have been a lot different going into the professional level, but it was hard for me to understand exactly how. In college, I averaged solid numbers. I played for the toughest coach. I brought skill, talent, and many other things to the table, and I did a lot for my team that didn't necessarily show up on the stat sheet. With energy and positivity, I did as much as I could for my team to help them look good as well as win games.

When I played with the Lady Vols, it was clear that we had great chemistry. We had one goal, and that was to win a title. Everyone knew their role on the team, and we trusted each other. Those factors played a major part in the Lady Vols' success. I guess that could be a reason why it was easier for me to be successful there than it is for me at the pro level, where a lot of politics, jealousy, selfishness, and lack of chemistry get in the way. As a pro overseas, it is hard to build a bond, because players are steadily competing against each other for fear of being outplayed and getting cut.

Every season, there are new faces on the team. You constantly had to learn how to play with one another and learn each other's strengths and weaknesses. Being the point guard is not for everyone, and it is not an easy role. Having been cut again, I had to find another job. Another Israeli team was looking for a point guard, and I agreed to finish out the season with the new team.

This new team was very bad; we lost every single game, but I was having fun and playing well. I was able to be Shannon Bobbitt on the court again instead of playing like a robot or worrying whether I was going to get cut after a few losses. The coach trusted and liked my game; we just weren't good enough as a team to win. I was able to become a scorer on this team—I had to score. That was a great challenge for me, because hardly anyone believed I could score. Scoring isn't an easy or sure thing for me; I just enjoy making my teammates happy and getting many assists. If I tried to score a lot, I felt I would be taking shots from my teammates whose job was to score. I didn't shoot the ball a lot every game; that wasn't my job, or my role on the team. I am a team player, and I try to be unselfish. To me, it didn't matter who did all of the scoring. I just cared about winning the game.

I enjoyed myself that season. I was happy to be on that team and enjoying life as a pro for once. After the season ended, I went home and did some thinking. I spoke to my family, and I decided to switch agents, because things weren't going how I would have liked them to go. I felt a change was necessary. We parted ways, and I found a new agent to represent me. It was nothing personal and there were no hard feelings; I simply made a decision that I felt would better my career.

# 10. BATTLEFIELD OF THOUGHTS

I was entering my fourth year in the 2011 WNBA season. In order to continue, I had to get offered to participate in a team training camp. I received an invitation and was happy that someone gave me another opportunity. I was ready to make this team, work hard, and compete. The world certainly works in mysterious ways, and everything—whether good or bad—happens for a reason. We just have to be ready to deal with the situations. The Indiana Fever chose to bring me to their training camp in order to see what I could bring to the team. I stayed in a hotel because I had to make the team before I could acquire more permanent accommodations.

The team already had two point guards, so I would actually be the third string point guard. It was a battle, but I loved playing and competing. I must admit, this time I was challenged and grew as a person and a player in a different way than I'd ever experienced before. I learned a lot about the league, specifically how to be a great point guard, and of course I also learned a lot about the game itself. I was chosen to be on the team by committee agreement. It came down to the last day or two before the final roster.

All of my faith and hard work paid off. I was happy to be back in the league. Through the Indiana Fever, I met one of the best players in the world: Tamika Catchings. She took me under her wing and taught me a lot about the business and about many other things in life. I watched her movements, and I was able to follow in her footsteps. We shared a very close relationship. She is an unbelievable player, and an even greater person. Catchings really showed her character through her actions. She worked hard every day in practice, and it showed in the games. I was like a sponge when I spent time with her. I always asked a lot of questions because that was the only way I was able to learn from my mistakes.

Training camp had been very hard; the coach was on me, and she made sure she pointed out my mistakes. She even asked me why I made certain decisions, telling me each time what a better decision would have been. She tested us on our plays so we could understand them better—the reason for running the play and who was getting the ball options out of each play. She even taught me rules about the game that I didn't know while playing in LA.

Even though I made the team, I wasn't complacent. I was ready for whatever was going to be thrown at me. I didn't know what to expect on any given day or at any given moment. I could have been cut; I was never guaranteed a place on the team. I had been cut so many times at that point that I was practically scared, almost expecting it to happen. Consequently, I never had a clear mind; I was always mentally down, and my confidence, in turn, was up and down. It was a lot of pressure for me because of the expectations that I had for myself and because of what I felt my family, friends, and fans expected of me.

When I made the team, I moved into my apartment. I was doing well in the practices and games, playing my role, but I still wasn't playing Bobbitt's game. I was playing like a robot because I was afraid of being cut. If any player that was playing against me wanted to outplay me, those years in the WNBA were the perfect time to do so, because I was holding myself back so much. My confidence was at an all-time low. I believe if I had been able to take full control of the game and play Bobbitt's basketball like Coach Summitt allowed me to do, there would not have been a guard that could hang with me, even at my height of five feet two inches. But instead, I was not being Bobbitt; I was barely playing, and I definitely wasn't showcasing my talent.

During training, players were so nervous that they didn't want to help me much because I was a threat. The players that did help me were players who weren't in my position or players who were guaranteed. It was shocking that players in my position were afraid to help me and teach me even though they were guaranteed to play for the team. I had to learn through my mistakes and find a way to look good. I was ready to have a great season and win a championship: my ultimate goal every year in the league. Being that I was third-string point guard, I typically didn't get much playing time. Still, I did my best to make the most of the minutes; I tried to stay ready, because God works in mysterious ways.

A day came when both point guards were injured at the same time. We had a game in my hometown. What were the chances of that happening? I became the starting point guard for that game, and not only did I play many minutes, I also played well. Even though we fell short, this game showed the value I brought to the team. I just had to always be ready.

The point guards were back to being healthy after that, and I went back to my role as third string. We made it to the eastern conference finals but fell short. We had many injuries that season, and we just couldn't get over that hump and close out games. I was mad that the teams I was a part of kept getting so close to victory but couldn't win a championship. I started to ask myself, was it because I wasn't able to bring more to the team? The season was over, and I had my exit meeting with the coaches and general manager. I was told the things I needed to work on, and I was happy with the meeting. I was looking forward to coming back to play with the Fever squad.

My new agent found me a job, and it was back in Turkey, just a different city—and therefore a different team. Since this was my second year playing in Turkey, I learned a little more of the language, and I was more familiar with the culture and style of play. This time around, I was not given a car, and I shared an apartment with two other players. While I didn't enjoy the city itself, practices were good. We had a packed crowd on game days; we were the city entertainment.

The poverty I witnessed while in Turkey made me appreciate America more. We have so much to be thankful for; our freedom culture, for one, and the list goes on. The Turkish people had strict rules, and many of them looked so angry and desperate at times, as if they had nothing to look forward to in life.

The city I was in had one big mall, but after awhile it became boring to go there to just eat and walk around. The other teams were hours away from my city, so there weren't really many people nearby to spend time with. When the weather was bad, my Internet would mess up, and all that was left to do

was read, write, sleep, or watch movies on my
computer.

Turkey is one of the most competitive countries in
which to play. I faced a great point guard in every
game, and every time I brought my best game.
Adding to the pressure to do well, fans and coaches
in Turkey bet on games. There was a lot of money
involved, which caused more stress and pressure to
handle. Still, I did my best to be my normal self and
have confidence while I was competing.

During my years overseas and my time playing for
different coaches, I found that everyone had a
different philosophy and tried to change the player I
was. But I only knew one way of playing, and that
was to play like Bobbitt and win! Mentally, I was
being challenged on every level, and it started to
make me think about my decision-making. I was
being cut left and right, and my confidence was
going down, and down, and down. The people in
my corner didn't allow me to succumb to my failure
and negative thinking, or even to criticism from

coaches. I had to remind myself how far I had come; how good I was as a player and a person; and that adversity was part of building my character for the bigger picture in life. I finished the season, realizing that I hadn't had many issues this time around. It was just another experience with lessons learned about people, my career, and life.

# 11. ON THE ROAD AGAIN

Entering my fifth year in the 2012 WNBA season, I was still with the Fever. I was anxious and excited to be coming back to a place where there was good team chemistry, and I was learning and growing as a person and player. It was time for me to compete for a starting position, or at the very least some playing time, and I still had the returning guards ahead of me. Teams hardly ever stay the same; there are always changes to be made when you lose, and sometimes even when you win. There are different reasons why teams make changes with the roster, and I knew I was never guaranteed on any team I played for.

I have worked hard for everything that I have had in basketball. For this reason, every achievement meant a lot to me, because it took hard work, blood, sweat, and tears, along with late nights and early mornings. When I returned to the Fever and was informed that I was being put back into a hotel, it immediately raised a red flag for me. My mind started wandering, thinking about all of the possible negative outcomes that a player in this position could possibly consider. Especially, after being on the team previously and having had an apartment. That was a sign I had to make the team again; I was so mad, and I couldn't really focus in practice, but I did the best I could to keep from thinking about having been put in the hotel. I called my family every night and explained to them how practices had gone and how I was feeling. I was doing my thing, but I still wasn't being Bobbitt. I had a strange feeling, but I was trying to brush it off and not think about it.

One day after practice, I remained on the court to shoot longer as I normally did while my teammates prepared to leave. I was shooting and thinking. As I looked around the arena I saw the general manager looking down at the team from the suite. I thought, "Today is the day someone will be cut." It was between me and another player, who happened to be a post player. She finally came down, and she and the coach were talking on the sideline, and then they left the gym and went into the office. A few minutes later, I was called to the office. Everyone in the gym at that time was staring at me as I left the court; they already knew what was happening.

I didn't even want to speak while I was in the office, listening to what the coach and manager had to say. I had been through this more than once, so I was familiar with it, and expecting it. My heart dropped and my eyes started to get watery, but I couldn't show them that I was crying and sad. During my talk with the coaches, they said that they needed to go in a different direction and that they needed a post player. They told me that I was great all throughout training camp and said it was a hard decision for them to make. But it was a business decision and they needed to have their roster sent to the main office. I thanked them for the opportunity, and I walked away and went to the hotel.

I called my parents, to whom I cried and vented to, and then I packed my bags. I was ready to fly home, but I didn't want the people at home to know I had gotten cut again. I stayed a few days in Indiana, still training and hanging with Catchings. She talked with me and calmed me down, and I felt a little better. I finally went home; I couldn't hide from my family and friends because the season was starting. They wouldn't see me on the bench or even on the roster, so everyone would have known either way that I had been cut from the team.

When I got home, I continued to work out and stay ready, because you never know when you will get a call. Still, I felt as if I were walking the hall of shame. I hoped for another opportunity to be in someone else's training camp, but training camps had ended for the season. Therefore, I wasn't able to show a team how I would be able to fit in or what I could bring to the table. There was no time for me to prove to the coaches that I was an asset to any team I might play with in the league. A few weeks would have to go by before the teams would feel like they needed to make changes—after losing several games.

I waited and waited, and then finally, a month into the season, I got a call from my agent. He told me that two teams were interested and that I should let him know which team I was interested in. After talking it over with my agent and my family, I decided to sign as a free agent with the Mystics. Excited and nervous at the same time, I packed my bags and made my way to DC.

I played in my first game with the Mystics, and guess who I played against? The Indiana Fever! Even though I didn't know any of the plays, I was ready to play that day. I knew just how to win against the Fever, and I was ready to prove people wrong once again. That's just what I did, and we won the game. Every time I got the ball I called for a pick and roll, and I picked the Fever defense apart. I knew I couldn't be guarded if I kept holding myself back mentally. My ball handling skills weren't normal; I played that game with a lot of energy and full-court-press defense, using my skills, talents, and speed to my advantage. I was happy about the outcome of the game; it had been a long time since I had felt good like that.

I was ready to learn about my teammates and the Mystics' system. I was happy another coach saw my ability and my potential—what I could bring to the team. Most of all, I was just happy to be in the league again, doing what I enjoyed. We had a rough season that year; we lost a lot of our games. We didn't have great chemistry, nor did we have many veterans that knew how to win and set the example. Collectively, we all had a number of team and individual weaknesses. I played as hard as I could and gave it all I had, but it wasn't enough.

My family came down to watch me play in person, and I showed them the DC life. Washington, DC is a nice city and has many historical sites. I didn't know much about the city. I did not have the opportunity to explore or learn about the city during my time there, because I had to focus on winning games. Most of my time was spent at home or hanging out with a few of my teammates.

The All Star break came around, and I was able to go home and hold my annual basketball clinic for the youth in my community. The kids were looking forward to seeing me and participating, and we had a great turnout once again. I wanted my clinic to grow and improve every year, so I reached out for donations and sponsorships so that the kids could have the best experience. This year I was able to get a gym donated, which helped tremendously because the weather was constantly changing. Some days it was raining, and other days it was too hot; I didn't want the kids to risk their health due to the weather conditions. The clinic was held outside the first year because I wanted the kids to experience basketball the way I did when I started. I wanted to show them how and where I trained to work on my game; I practiced every day outside. For the clinic this year, however, the conditions were certainly not ideal.

After the clinic, I went back to DC to start the second half of the season and try to turn the season around to win some games with the Mystics. We struggled more in the second half than we had in the first; we couldn't win games, and we finished the season with the worst record in the history of the WNBA. I had my exit meeting, and then I was on my way home to relax with my family. I was able to buy my daddy a car and help my mommy pay her bills. I love to help them and make sure they are taken care of, because they have done so much for me. Whenever I have needed them, they have been there to comfort me.

Entering my fifth year overseas, I was excited about playing again in Turkey because I had sat out the whole summer. However, the economy was not going well overseas. Every team budget was low, and many teams didn't have much money to pay their players. Some countries required a certain number of foreigners on each team, and teams in Turkey were allowed three to four American players each.

As soon as I arrived in my city after a long flight with layovers, I went to get a physical so I could be cleared to play. Once again, I had to adjust to the time change. This year I had my own apartment but was not given a car, so I had to walk everywhere or take a taxi depending on how far I was going. I didn't live far from restaurants or the gym, and I loved the facility. It had everything you could think of in one building: weight room, sauna, steam room, pool, courts, film room, and game room. Everything I needed was available to me.

This season I didn't go home for Christmas break. I wasn't ready to fly home on a long flight and then a few days later fly right back to Turkey, so I stayed, trained, watched games, and relaxed a little. I became more of a tourist in Turkey that year. I took more pictures and learned more about the culture and people; I went to the movies, the mall, and walked around the city. My experience there was a good one, and I shared my stories with family and friends who may never get the opportunity to go abroad.

My team was solid that season, and we were one game short from making the playoffs. One of the things I disliked most about playing on the low-budget teams was the traveling. One of the trips I experienced was driving with my team on a bus for twelve hours to reach our destination. It was miserable. I read, did some writing, watched a movie, listened to music, and we still had a few more hours to go. That trip was very uncomfortable, and as soon as we got to the city, we had practice. As the season drew to a close, I had my last few days in Turkey, said my farewells, and headed to the airport to catch my flight back to the States.

# 12. LESSONS BEFORE BLESSINGS

After a horrible season the previous year, the Mystics made some changes in their roster for both coaches and players going into the 2013 season. I spoke with the new coach before I went to DC, asking him if he wanted me on the team; how he viewed me as a player; and what he expected from me. The coach told me to be myself, work on hitting the open shots, improve my floater, and be a pest on defense. I felt good about our conversation. The coach spoke very highly of the upcoming WNBA season and me; I was included in the team plans.

It was a different story when I made it to training camp, however. The coach had made some changes, and he not only traded for a point guard, but also drafted another point guard. Immediately I knew that my job was on the line. I tried to ignore the negative talk in my mind so I wouldn't lose focus, and I continued to control what I could control— and that was me working hard to prove I was a great player and how I could help the team win a championship.

Still, the thought that I might be cut wasn't so easy to ignore. This was my livelihood; my job. I was not getting the proper opportunity from the coaches; it was as if they already knew the team roster. Even in practice, the coaches weren't really trying to teach me exactly what they wanted from me as a point guard, and when the teams were set up, I was always on the team with the players that were not going to make the roster. This saying is so true: "Self-doubt and fear are more dangerous than failure itself." My chances of making the team were very slim, but I stayed as a professional should, and I worked hard every day. I even tried to give advice to the rookies on my team. I didn't care if they played my position or not; I was comfortable in my game.

The days were counting down. We had team media pictures, but I was excluded from certain photos and certain interviews. Then the day came when the final roster had to be sent to the main office. I had just finished lifting weights, and one of the post players had just gotten cut. I was sad and nervous for myself, and as I was walking down the hallway, I was told that the coach wanted to speak to me. Instantly, I knew what the talk was going to be about. I didn't really want to talk, but I went to hear what he had to say. He said he had decided to go in a different direction because his original plans didn't work out. I had so many questions and concerns, but I didn't feel it was necessary to discuss them; I knew he had made up his mind.

I thanked the coaches and left the office. Devastated, I called my parents and told them I was ready to quit. They calmed me down and gave me great advice. They said that people in the higher levels have hard decisions to make and sometimes make mistakes, too, and that is what life is about—facing obstacles and learning how to bounce back; not staying down, but continuing to stay strong and not give up.

I packed my bags and left the same day. My parents drove to DC to pick me up, and I was happy that I was only three hours away from home. As we headed north, I thought about my future and tried to understand why I was getting cut from these teams, wondering what I could do to fix the issue. I knew my height and politics both played roles in why I kept getting cut. I had given my all at every single training camp; injuries weren't an issue, and neither was money. It was timing, and finding a coach that would believe in me and let me be my natural self on the court.

When I finally made it home, I took some time to relax and calm my nerves. Then I got right back into training as I waited for another opportunity in the league. I was also happy to be able to host my third basketball clinic, and that was the first year I began offering the clinic to girls only. I called it the Shannon Bobbitt "Lady Phenoms." I taught young ladies about self-esteem and confidence, showing them how to carry themselves, and encouraging them to be the best they could be in life.

I did a few speaking engagements for other clinics and schools throughout NYC that summer. I went back to my alma mater, the University of Tennessee, and visited with my coaches and worked out for a few weeks. The end of the summer was drawing near, and I still hadn't received any word from my agent about a team wanting me in the WNBA, or even overseas. This really caused me to question my ability and lose my self-confidence.

Sitting out a second year in a row from the WNBA was becoming depressing. Fall came and went, and though I received no calls, I continued to train. I called my agent and thanked them, but told them I no longer needed their services. I was now without a job and an agent, and while I was thankful that I had had those experiences overseas and happy that I had continued to work hard, I was frustrated and worried about my career.

Finally, I was contacted for a job in Turkey, for the same team as before, with the same goals. The team had a low budget, but I had to make a move in order to generate income, build my confidence back up, and play to get ready for another opportunity in the WNBA. My Turkish friend helped me get this job overseas, and I was happy to play again. Sometimes seeing the big picture is hard; you can't see the picture when you're in the frame. I knew I had worked hard, but I wasn't where I wanted to be in my basketball career. I wanted to continue to prove people wrong and show everyone that I was one of the best point guards to play the game.

The Turkish team was in a bad spot; they had a terrible record. It was an easy transition to come onto the team; I knew the coaches and a few of the players. The team was young, inexperienced, and lacked chemistry. The worst team in the Turkish league, they had only won a few games and so they were forced to go to second division. On top of that, the team was experiencing money issues toward the end of the season and had trouble paying their players on time. It was all a bad combination: not winning and not getting paid, and overall not being happy.

I did a lot of soul searching about myself as a person and a player that season. On the bright side, I was a fan favorite everywhere I played. I even spoke to a few high school students in Turkey, sharing my story and experience in basketball. I was excited and honored to speak. Having the opportunity to share my story—to inspire and motivate others—is my ultimate goal in life.

## 13. FOUL PLAY

I was now entering my seventh year overseas as a professional athlete, and I decided to take my talents back to Poland. WNBA players usually start coming overseas in October, but this year, for the first time, I came early. Since I was out of the league for the second year in a row, it was time for me to start making money and playing again. I regretted coming early, though. The team was an up-and-coming team, and we practiced two times a day, kept long hours, and even ran outside in the park and woods.

I had my own apartment this time, though it was not fully furnished, and I shared a car with two other Americans. This was the first year I played on a team that would drive two to six hours on game day and play—something very different from what I was used to.

My second time in Poland, I decided to branch out more. I decided to meet people, talk more, network, and learn the language. Overall, it was a rough experience. My teammates were cool; we weren't a great team, but we worked hard. We lost our first three games, so that made my stay there even harder. The city was very small and quiet, and there wasn't much to do in the way of entertainment. So most nights overseas I entertained myself by writing, reading, sleeping, and talking both on the phone and on Skype. I also watched movies and played chess. I counted down the days until Christmas, when I could fly home and spend time with my family.

When I came home from Poland after that long, rough season, I was so exhausted that I had to take a break. I went without touching a ball for an entire month, though I still watched basketball films, went to games, and stayed in shape—just in other ways.

The last team I had played with, as I mentioned before, was in a financial situation, and therefore running behind on paying me my last month's salary, which they ultimately paid about two months later. That was the risk you took for playing overseas, but there were rewards, too: the experience, playing against and meeting new people, and learning things—these are priceless.

I started to network a lot more, because being in and out of the league, I wasn't sure if my WNBA career was looking too bright. I gave back to the youth more, training kids almost every day—this time, both boys and girls. I created a "Shannon Bobbitt Learn the Basic Steps Fundamental Basketball Handbook" for the youth to study and learn the game. I hosted my usual clinic as well. In fact, I did two that summer.

The WNBA season was just around the corner; I needed someone to represent me to get in the league, so I reached out to my first agent for representation. From the 2013 season to the 2015 season, I stayed out the entire time. I continued to work hard, teach the youth, and spend time with my family. I didn't have much of a personal, fun life, because I knew the "fun" could distract me, and I would never bounce back if I lost my focus. My priorities were to concentrate on my dream and goals for basketball and know that the fun would come soon enough. I didn't play in any street ball tournaments, because I simply didn't enjoy them anymore. I also didn't want to get hurt—then I'd really not have another opportunity in the league. I stayed ready, but my confidence was up and down because of being cut left and right. Spending time with family and close friends during that time was great for me.

I grew over the summer—mentally, spiritually, and physically. I still didn't know why other players had been chosen over me, but I knew I wanted to be back in the league, and I took comfort in knowing that my teammates respected me and my game. Despite the tough circumstances, I knew my resume spoke for itself: I was a champion, a good point guard, and a team player. Perhaps it was simply politics; if it was, I wondered why they hadn't been on my side.

I enjoyed my summer for the most part. I considered it to be productive, because I was able to act as a mentor for others; network for life after basketball; and of course spend time with my loved ones. I was waiting to see where I would be heading for my seventh season overseas.

I played my seventh year overseas in Poland once more, sharing a hotel room with two other people, the three of us also sharing one car. As for games, we were zero and seven—we just couldn't seem to find a way to win. At one point, I came down with a cold and a fever. My coach's girlfriend, who was also my teammate, brought me some medicine and some Vitamin C. The medicine made me feel a little better, but I was still tired and weak.

At first I wasn't going to play in the game, but I decided to give it a try, playing against my better judgment. During the game, I wasn't my normal self. The second half came, and I told the trainer I was feeling weak; he said he would tell the coach. We were only down by seven points. The team we were playing was not better than us; we could have and should have won. It was at our home, in front of our fans.

Throughout the second half, we were missing shots, turning the ball over, playing bad defense— everything was going badly, and we ended up losing the game by seventeen points. The coach came in the locker room and said that no matter how sick he was, he would never give up on his team. He walked out of the locker room and slammed the door. Our coach blamed me for the loss—I couldn't believe it.

I was feeling extremely sick and frustrated at the same time. I wanted to talk with him. Even though I was sick, I was still upset that I hadn't been able to play in the game. The coach seemed to feel that I had given up on the team, but I had given all I had. I wasn't helping my team in that condition—I was simply feeling too weak mid-game, and my health always will come first.

After the game, the fans were chanting and screaming to fire the coach. It was very bad. The coach wasn't the greatest coach, but he tried to change some things for the better—only nothing was working. While in Poland, I was unhappy and uncomfortable; I knew I needed to leave to be on another team and in another country.

Again, the team was weeks late paying my salary; I continued to play for a while, but I was waiting on my payment. Eventually I contacted my agent and explained the situation. I informed her that I wouldn't be attending practice or playing in the games anymore, because at that point, two months of my salary had yet to be paid. This was something I never imagined I would have to do—not go to practice or games—but this industry is a business like any other, and I hadn't come overseas to play for free.

My accomplishments gave me the recognition, respect, and confidence that I had always sought. They showed me that working hard has sweet rewards in the end. More than my accomplishments, the obstacles that I faced made me a positive woman and a better role model for those younger than me. I am now able to take care of my family, and even help others make a difference in their own lives.

I never wanted to be the woman who said I could've, should've, but didn't. I wanted to make my dreams come true and share my story. I look forward to doing even greater things, because I know that determination and a little belief can take you very far.

One lesson I learned on my journey is that my competition was not the players I went up against every day on the court, the coaches, or the people who didn't believe in me. It was the person looking back at me in the mirror every day. I realized that I was holding my self back. I was my own competition, and had I not been careful I could have become my own worst enemy.

My dream was fulfilled. Yours can be, as well. I played on the biggest stage, as the smallest player, to accomplish my goals. If I encouraged you even a "Lil Bit" to have the spirit and willpower to go after what you want, then my story has served its purpose.

# EPILOGUE

I was once a little girl growing up on the streets of Harlem with a height disadvantage and with all the odds faced against me, and now here I am with a story to tell. I won back-to-back national titles under a legendary coach and played along side great players throughout the world. I also was player of year and titled hall of famer in Trinity Valley.

When the announcer stepped up to the podium and said, "With the fifteenth pick, the Los Angeles Sparks select Shannon Bobbitt from the University of Tennessee," that was a priceless moment that no one can ever take away from me.

The average height of a WNBA player is about five-feet-eight inches. My chances of making it to league were low standing at five-foot-two. But I made it!

I was able to become a successful WNBA player, not because I was the tallest or smartest on the court, but because during the days when it was raining or snowing, and during the times I was tired and weak, I forced myself to work on my craft—to be the best point guard I could be.

Accomplishing my goal wasn't easy; it took dedication, discipline, spiritual strength, and I worked harder than you can imagine. Everything that happened on and off the court, whether good, bad, or ugly, has allowed me to be the person I am today. Being a person of strength, faith, and determination, I am optimistic about my future and unexpected battles to come. I am proud to say that my life experiences have taught me to be fearless.

I wanted to make sure I became successful, because I wanted to prove people wrong, for one thing. I easily could have given up and stopped chasing my dream, but I stayed strong. I would never say that the journey was simple and sweet—in fact, it was like a storm, constantly wreaking havoc. I could have waited for the storm to pass before I continued working towards my goal, but instead, I learned how to turn adversity into strength—something you can do, too.

You can believe in yourself ninety-nine percent, but that final one percent could make a difference and turn your entire life around!

On October 24, 2015, Bobbitt was inducted into the
Trinity Valley Lady Cardinals Hall of Fame.

# ADDITIONAL FOREWORDS

Up until the 2006-07 basketball season, there had been only one player since 1977 that had joined the University of Tennessee women's basketball program as a junior college transfer. Just prior to that 2006-07 season, our coaching staff agreed to break with tradition and pursue two such players.

One of those targeted recruits was Shannon Denise Bobbitt, a five-foot-two stick of dynamite from New York, who could break ankles with her crossover move as well as hit an open teammate with a bullet pass, or score on a layup or via a long-range three. In a decision that would prove fortuitous for the Lady Volunteers, Shannon finished her associate degree and highly successful basketball career at Trinity Valley Community College in Athens, Texas, and signed scholarship papers to play for Tennessee.

In our staff's experience, recruiting junior college players sometimes comes with risks. Players might have skill limitations, academic challenges, or character issues. They also may struggle adapting to a new head coach or program, especially one with the high expectations instilled by Hall of Fame coach, Pat Summitt. Many times it takes players a year or two to get comfortable at the NCAA Division I level, and it usually just made more sense to have a player with four years of eligibility to adjust as opposed to having only two years, as a junior college player.

We knew Shannon was a great person and an outstanding player. She had averaged 16.4 points and 7.5 assists per game, and was selected the 2006 Women's Basketball Coaches Association (WBCA) Junior Community College Player of the Year. She also earned All-America honors. What we didn't know was how big of a heart she had, and how quickly she would make an impact.

The answers to those unknowns were huge and immediate. Shannon was the starting point-guard in all seventy-four games she played for Tennessee during her two-year career, and she led our program to back-to-back NCAA National Championships in 2006-07 and 2007-08. Yes, we had a future Olympian and No. 1 WNBA draft pick in Candace Parker on that squad, but it took a unified team to bring home the hardware, and Shannon was our floor general.

She averaged 9.3 points, 3.0 assists, 2.3 rebounds and 1.6 steals per game in those seventy-four starts, and she also shot eighty percent from the free throw line and nearly forty-one percent from the three-point arc. Those statistics certainly contributed to Tennessee winning seventy games—and losing only five—during her time at Rocky Top, but it was her leadership that made the difference.

When she arrived, there was something our team desperately needed but didn't have, and that was a point guard who could run the team and be a coach on the floor. Shannon filled that void. She also brought energy to our team, making up for any size she lacked with a huge, huge heart.

Being a junior college transfer, Shannon had to come in like she had been in this program for two years. It was a challenge for her. She had to stay later, do all of the little things, put in the time, and learn the system—and she did.

Shannon exemplified what being a Lady Vol is all about. She didn't back down from one challenge—not one. Whether it was in the weight room, on the court, or in the classroom, she faced everything with strong determination and fought through any adversity that came her way. She helped others do the same.

She was a blue-collar worker, and she brought everyone on the team along with her, helping make our program stronger. Our team rallied around her, and the results on the court demonstrated that.

After first going to junior college and then spending two years in our program, Shannon was drafted by the WNBA's Los Angeles Sparks. She realized her long-time goal of playing professional basketball was coming into existence. Shannon had some hurdles along her journey, but she didn't let those deter her from living her dreams of playing for national championships and being on the biggest stage in women's basketball. She simply wouldn't be denied.

It's that combination of ambition, character, loyalty, tenacity, and work ethic—the hallmarks of a true Lady Vol—that make Shannon Bobbitt a champion on the court, and a winner in the game of life.

*Holly Warlick*
*Head Women's Basketball Coach*
*University of Tennessee*

Breakfast and a phone call—those two items put Shannon Bobbitt on the radar screen of the Tennessee Lady Vols. Shannon's high school coach, Ed Grezinsky, was working our Elite Camp, and he and I had struck up a friendship. We were having breakfast one morning, and he told me about one of his former players from Murry Bergtraum High School who was attending Trinity Valley Community College in Texas. During our breakfast, Ed gave me a description of Shannon's game, and some of her attributes as a competitor.

At that very moment, in June 2005, we had a full stable of guards, and we had already received a verbal commitment from a good high school senior guard. Fast forward a few months to December 2005, and we'd just learned one of our point guards was going to transfer and leave Tennessee. This was unbeknownst to Ed, and he called me two days after we had learned about the player transferring…so the timing was incredible! Ed again extolled Shannon's virtues and really assured me that Shannon was the "real deal" and could flat-out play.

I remembered our breakfast conversation back in June, and the doors began to open up.

So in January 2006, I flew to Texas to watch Shannon and her team practice. Now, our coaching staff placed a high value on Ed's word and recommendation. However, the primary concern was Shannon's height; she was listed at five feet three inches, but some coaches said she was barely five foot two—pretty short for SEC-caliber point guards. I remember her practice so clearly; the team began with some fundamental drills and warm-ups, and Shannon looked pretty good.

Eventually, the team worked on breaking a man-to-man full-court press with traps and random double teams. The real kicker was that the Trinity Valley coaches had some football players, primarily wide receivers and defensive backs, as practice players who were pressing and trapping. There were four of them that day, all playing at once, and the only player who they could not contain, let alone put in any kind of trap, was Shannon Bobbitt. Her quickness, ball-handling skills, vision, court awareness, and overall toughness were impressive—and that made me an instant believer! Coach Summitt and I went to one of her junior college tournament games at the end of Shannon's season, and Coach Summitt was sold, as well. Shannon ended up a junior college All-American, the junior college Player of the Year, and after a highly competitive recruiting battle, we were fortunate that she decided to attend the University of Tennessee!

Well, history has recorded the rest of the story. Shannon came in, earned a starting position with our team, and went on to help us win consecutive NCAA National Championships in 2007 and 2008. She was everything Ed had described in our previous conversations, and then some. Shannon had exceptional ball-handling skills; she was a fearless competitor and could really bring tremendous defensive energy and pressure. Coach Summitt's brand of discipline and accountability took some getting used to for Shannon at first, but she adjusted well, and bought into all aspects of our program.

Above all else, Shannon was a true competitor in every phase of her life, and she wanted to win. It would have been easy for Shannon to come in with some attitude and self-centeredness after her junior college accomplishments, but that wasn't who she was. Shannon came in, saw the talent around her, and recognized immediately the possibility of winning championships. Instead of making it about her, Shannon made it about the team, and she quickly carved out a role for herself and embraced that role fully.

Coming out of Trinity Valley, Shannon was not a consistent perimeter shooter from the arc; however, she spent hours in the gym working on and improving her shot. Not only did she become much more consistent, but Shannon hit some huge three-point shots in the 2007 National Championship game to help us achieve victory. She was a relentless worker who strove to be her absolute best;

she was not afraid of putting in extra time and work to continue her improvement.

Shannon was also very coachable and receptive. There was nothing she wouldn't do if it meant bringing our team closer to a championship. As a result of this level of commitment, Shannon became one of only two players in Lady Vol's history to win a National Championship in each season she wore Tennessee orange—and that's a pretty special achievement.

As a player, Shannon provided the extra ingredient we needed to win national championships. She went on to enjoy a very successful career in the WNBA and overseas, but what truly makes Shannon special is her indomitable spirit and her will to persevere. Shannon has overcome challenges and hardships along the way, silencing critics and doubters who said she couldn't do it. She has shown the will of a champion to move past or through any challenge she has faced, and not merely to survive, but to thrive. By putting in an immense amount of extra time and work, Shannon not only improved her game; she also graduated on time from the University of Tennessee, which was very hard to do as a transfer student. Simply put, Shannon Bobbitt has the heart of a true champion in life, and she is a great teammate, daughter, and friend.

Hopefully you will be encouraged and inspired as you read Shannon's story and experience her determination, strength, and resolve to succeed. I know you will learn from Shannon how to press on through adversity and challenges. Shannon Bobbitt was a real "difference-maker" for the Tennessee Lady Vols, and her story can be helpful to anyone in life who is pursuing excellence. Shannon is a living testimony that great things can come in small packages! I wish you as much enjoyment reading her book as we had in coaching her at Tennessee.

*Dean Lockwood*
*Assistant Women's Basketball Coach*
*University of Tennessee*

In April 2007, I remember watching Shannon hit four three-pointers in the championship game to win the seventh title for the Lady Vols—big shot after big shot, and a couple of kick outs in the corner…a skip pass from the other wing, and one in transition. Most people assume the starting point guard for the University of Tennessee would be a good perimeter shooter, and Shannon was. But most people didn't know where she started from, and what she had done to become who she is now.

I had the good fortune to coach Shannon during her freshman and sophomore years at Trinity Valley Community College. We were able to recruit her out of high school, because she wanted more exposure and better opportunities than some of the smaller Division I's that had been recruiting her. We thought she had a great skillset, was a tremendous ball handler, a great passer, and possessed speed as well as a confidence in her game that went well beyond her five-foot-nothing size. However, she had a major weakness in her game that she knew she had to develop if she wanted to reach her basketball goals and dream.

Shannon arrived on campus at TVCC about ten days before the fall semester of her freshman year began. She wanted to come in early and start developing and improving her game. I do not think it is an exaggeration to say that when she first arrived, her shooting range was limited to about four feet. Any shots other than a layup were a bit off target, to say the least. One of the things that separated Shannon from others, though, was that she realized her weakness and was willing to put in the time and effort to change that.

For those first ten days before school started, she lived in the gym. We worked on her shooting form and motion. We started in front of the rim at about three feet. She put up thousands of shots before we would let her move back another step. Those individual shooting sessions continued on throughout her two years. By the end of her freshman year, she had become a great shooter to about fifteen feet. As a sophomore, she extended her range to become a threat behind the arc. It wasn't by chance; it was because of the time, effort, and commitment Shannon made, taking her game to another level.

In April 2007 (and again in April 2008), while most fans applauded and cheered for the Lady Vols for winning the NCAA Championship, I was so proud of Shannon because of the hours, months, and years she had spent in the gym, positioning herself to seize the moment when the opportunity presented itself. Most do not know where she started and the commitment she made to be able to accomplish all the things she has thus far in her career. Job well done.

*Michael Landers*
*Head Men's Basketball Coach*
*Navarro College*

# ABOUT THE AUTHOR

SHANNON BOBBITT is a lady phenomenon who faced many obstacles throughout her life. With her work ethic, positive attitude, and inspiring determination, she is able to triumph all battles. Bobbitt is a humble, warm-hearted philanthropist who loves to put smiles on others' faces, and she hopes one day to run her own recreational facility for youth. In her spare time, Shannon enjoys spending time with loved ones and friends, and she also gives private and group basketball—and life—

lessons. Bobbitt is working on producing her own documentary. She currently resides in New York City.